QUEST FOR QUALITY

JOINT COMMISSION ON CRIMINOLOGY AND CRIMINAL JUSTICE EDUCATION AND STANDARDS

HARRY E. ALLEN
San Jose State University

LARRY R. BASSI
SUNY-Brockport

JULIUS DEBRO
Former Principal Investigator
Atlanta University

GEORGE T. FELKENES
Long Beach State University

EDITH FLYNN
Northeastern University

GORDON E. MISNER
A.C.J.S. Alternate
University of Illinois-Chicago

C. RAY JEFFERY
Florida State University

WILLIAM J. MATHIAS
University of South Carolina

RICHTER H. MOORE JR.
Appalachian State University

FRANK SCARPITTI
University of Delaware

RICHARD H. WARD
Project Director
University of Illinois-Chicago

VINCENT J. WEBB
Principal Investigator
University of Nebraska at Omaha

CHARLES WELLFORD
A.S.C. Alternate
University of Maryland

PROJECT STAFF AND ASSISTANTS

Ora Allen, Word Processing; Nancy A. Hirsch, Administrative Assistant; Rona Hitlin, Accountant; Carolyn Johnson, Research Associate; Barbara Leahy, Research Assistant; Seth Lerer, Senior Writer; Scott Marden, Research Associate; Mary Pallen, Administrative Aide; Elizabeth M. Sebuck, Senior Research Associate; Beatrix A. Siman, Senior Research Associate; Janice Smith, Administrative Aide; Julie A. Staszak, Administrative Assistant; Sheryl S. Taylor, Research Assistant; Vicky S. Vasquez, Administrative Aide, and Claire Villarreal, Senior Administrative Assistant.

STUDENT ASSISTANTS

Caroline Anigbo, Charles Burack, Sandy Buckley, Michael Collier, Miguel Dabul, Julianne Felkner, Gustavo Guzman, Kamal Hammouda, Ken Holland, Patti Jacobsen, Panorea Lekkas, Sheryl Lynn Leventhal, Steve Mihajlovic, Barbara Montefel, Amy Moskowitz, Lois F. Owrutsky, Daniel Payne, Rebecca L. Rawa, Angela Shelton, Lorie Smith, Mark D. Steinberg, and Darlene Turner.

QUEST FOR QUALITY

PRINCIPAL AUTHORS:

Richard H. Ward
University of Illinois at Chicago

Vincent J. Webb
University of Nebraska at Omaha

*A Publication
of the Joint Commission
on Criminology and Criminal Justice
Education and Standards*

University Publications
New York

Prepared under Grant Number 79CD-AX-0001
from the Office of Criminal Justice Education and Training,
Law Enforcement Assistance Administration,
U.S. Department of Justice,
under the Omnibus Crime Control and Safe
Streets Act of 1968, as amended.

Points of view or opinions in this document do
not necessarily represent the official position
or policies of the U.S. Department of Justice.

Library of Congress Cataloging in Publication Data
Ward, Richard H.
  Quest for Quality.

  Bibliography: p.
  Includes index.
  1. Criminal justice, Administration of--Study and
teaching (Higher)--United States. 2. Criminal justice,
Administration of--Study and teaching (Higher)--Standards
--United States. I. Webb, Vincent J. II. Joint
Commission on Criminology and Criminal Justice Education
and Standards (U.S.) III. Title.
HV9950.W37   364'.07'1173   84-7208
ISBN 0-911463-01-1
  Manufactured in the United States of America.

TABLE OF CONTENTS

PREFACE

Fifteen years ago congress enacted the Omnibus Crime Control and Safe Streets Act which provided the authorization for establishing the Law Enforcement Assistance Administration (L.E.A.A.) in the Department of Justice. In the years that followed, the federal government has had a major influence on the field of criminal justice through the provision of funds for a broad range of programs, from research regarding the causes of crime to direct assistance for support of operational activities in cities and states all across the nation.

One of the most interesting and significant aspects of this period was the assistance provided in the general field of human resources development, especially as related to programs in higher education. Because of L.E.A.A. assistance, largely through the Law Enforcement Education Program (L.E.E.P.), crime-related programs in higher education increased from a handful in the late sixties to well over 1000 in the mid-seventies.

This sudden attention to crime-related higher education, although welcomed by everyone, was accompanied by some serious concerns and perplexing questions concerning issues ranging from the goals educators should have, and the boundaries and definitions of the field, to the quality of the program and how to measure that quality.

Criminological and criminal justice educators had been increasingly concerned about these problems since the sixties and many saw a need to develop minimum standards for educational programs. L.E.A.A.'s administrator, Richard W. (Pete) Velde, understood the far reaching significance of L.E.E.P. as well as other educational and human resource development programs he supported. However, he also had concerns regarding the same issues which bothered educators in the field. Therefore, in 1976, he established the Office of Criminal Justice Education and Training (O.C.J.E.T.) to provide an organizational capability to focus resources and attention on meeting the challenges, realizing the opportunities, and addressing the concerns which were emerging.

That event marked the beginning of a five year period in which many challenges were met, opportunities were realized, and concerns of the field were addressed. However, this is not the whole story. In fact, one of the most significant aspects relates to a successful, meaningful partnership which grew out of a mutual concern of the federal bureaucracy and academia regarding policy oriented research. The Joint Commission on Criminology and Criminal Justice Education and Standards represents one of the clearest examples in which this partnership was successful! In fact the publication of this final report of the Commission, with the impact it has already had and will continue to have on the field is sufficient evidence of this success story.

History will certainly confirm that one of L.E.A.A.'s most significant contributions to the criminology and criminal justice field was its educational programs, and the Joint Commission on Criminology and Criminal Justice Education and Standards will be recognized as one of its most significant projects. Certainly, the leadership of the Academy of Criminal Justice Sciences and the American Society of Criminology deserve special recognition for their vision and support in accelerating the processes of evolution to bring a maturity to the field which, by normal expectations, would have probably occurred in the next century.

—J. Price Foster
University of Louisville
Former Director of the Office of Criminal
Justice Education and Training (L.E.A.A.)

FOREWORD

Publication of this report of the Joint Commission on Criminology and Criminal Justice Education and Standards marks the culmination of almost five years of work covering a broad range of activities and research. This book has been designed to provide answers to many perplexing questions that have plagued criminal justice education almost from its inception. The Joint Commission on Criminology and Criminal Justice Education and Standards was formed due to the efforts of several members of the American Society of Criminology (A.S.C.) and the Academy of Criminal Justice Sciences (A.C.J.S.). These individuals saw a need for minimum standards within the field. Although many leaders in criminal justice education perceived problems with the quality of many criminal justice programs, they disagreed on the best way to cope with them. A series of discussions were initiated in the early 1970's between Dr. Price Foster, then Director of the Office of Criminal Justice Education and Training (O.C.J.E.T.) of the Law Enforcement Assistance Administration, and members of A.S.C. and A.C.J.S., As successive presidents of A.C.J.S. in 1975 and 1976, Dr. George Felkenes and Dr. Gordon Misner played major roles in some of these discussions. Dr. William Amos, who was president of A.S.C., also contributed much to these early discussions, as did Dr. Charles Wellford.

During the tenure of Dr. Richard Ward as president of A.C.J.S., Dr. Foster brought a group of educators and practitioners to Washington to explore the feasibility of a grant to develop minimum standards for criminal justice education and to explore issues related to the implementation of standards. The grant proposal was reworked and revised by Dr. Ward and Dr. Wellford, working with drafts originally submitted by Dr. Misner and Dr. Felkenes.

A grant was awarded to the Academy of Criminal Justice Sciences in October, 1977 with the understanding that A.C.J.S. would collaborate with ASC through a joint advisory board. Dr. Richard Ward, then Vice President for Administration at John Jay College of Criminal Justice, was named Project Director, and four individuals from each of the professional associations were appointed to the Board. The Board ultimately established itself as the Joint Commission on Criminology and Criminal Justice Education and Standards. During the course of the initial and subsequent grants, the Commission developed the research methodology and the minimum standards in this report.

The first meeting of the group was held in November, 1977. The following representatives of A.S.C. attended; C. Ray Jeffery, Donal E.J. MacNamara, Charles Newman, and Charles Wellford. With the election of a new A.S.C. administration, the following members were asked to continue to serve: Harry E. Allen, San Jose State University; Larry R. Bassi, S.U.N.Y.-Brockport; George T. Felkenes, Long Beach State University; Edith Flynn, Northeastern University; C. Ray Jeffery, Florida State University; William J. Mathias, University of South Carolina; Richter H. Moore, Jr., Appalachian State University; and Frank Scarpitti, University of Delaware.

Initially, the project offices were housed in Washington, D.C., and Dr. Julius Debro was appointed by the Commission to serve as Principal Investigator. In 1977, Dr. Ward was appointed Vice Chancellor for Administration at the University of Illinois in Chicago. As a result, a decision was made to move the project to Chicago and to house it in the Center for Research in Law and Justice at the University of Illinois. During this period Dr. Vincent Webb of the University of Nebraska at Omaha was appointed to serve as the Principal Investigator.

The number of people who made important contributions to the Joint Commission's efforts exceeds our ability to name them here. At the risk of omitting any of those individuals, the

Joint Commission would like to express its appreciation to authors of monographs published by the Commission, contributors to the methodology and research effort, and many of the subcontractors who were a part of the project. For a list of monograph authors and others who served as consultants or contributors to the project, see Appendix III.

We are particularly indebted to those researchers and authors who preceded us and whose contributions provide much of the framework upon which this report is based. Three specific studies are worthy of mention: the National Manpower Survey of the Criminal Justice System, funded by the Law Enforcement Assistance Administration, particularly Volume V on Higher Education for which Jim Stinchcomb of Virginia Commonwealth University had responsibility; the report of the National Advisory Commission on Higher Education for Police Officers, particularly the work of Dr. Lawrence Sherman of the State University of New York at Albany; and a report from John Jay College, *Criminal Justice Education: The End of the Beginning,* which was supervised by Dean Richard Pearson. All of these individuals readily assisted in the efforts of the Joint Commission, and their efforts engendered many of the ideas presented here.

With respect to the minimum standards in this report, the Commission chose to draw upon many recommendations for standards from prior reports, especially those in the Sherman report and those developed by A.C.J.S. Many remain in their original form; others have been reworded in light of recent developments. The standards within this report have been read by a wide range of practitioners and educators and have received widespread support. The Commission considered a thorough reading essential if the report is to be valuable in the future development of criminal justice education.

Much of the data in the report confirm the conclusions of earlier reports. Probably the most significant aspects of the Joint Commission's effort have been toward developing baseline data and toward answering long unanswered questions.

Encouraging changes have taken place in criminal justice higher education in the past decade, many of them in the past few years. The Commission found, however, a number of concerns which must be addressed by the field if it is to achieve the level of quality toward which it professes to aspire. It is hoped this report will initiate discussion and debate and make a contribution toward change. Criminal justice educators cannot be complacent about past changes and achievements, because we continue to face many of the problems which gave rise to criminal justice higher education.

The standards presented in this report are minimal, and represent a starting point rather than an ideal.

Initially the Joint Commission set as its goal a comprehensive research effort that would address both primary and secondary considerations related to criminal justice higher education. As a result, the Commission produced ten monographs, several theses and working papers, and a wealth of data. This report attempts to relate the Commission's efforts to one another. The serious student of criminal justice higher education should become familiar with the reports that preceded this one, as well as the project monographs and other publications of the Commission.

This report has not been an easy project, and strife and dissension have occurred among many individuals who helped prepare it for publication. Dissension is not unusual, for the topic is a volatile one to Commission members and many others who represented a wide range of views. Nevertheless, the Commission was unanimous in its agreement concerning standards. Many members felt that the standards were too restrictive or narrow in focus; in some cases, members felt that the standards were too broad and went beyond the scope of being minimum. For the most part, a consensus was established through long and tedious argument and discussion, but there was a consensus.

The authors are indebted to a great many individuals who provided support in various ways. We would like to thank Seth Lerer of Princeton University who spent the summer of 1981 assisting in the editing and rewriting phase of the project. His contribution has been invaluable and significant. Dr. Donald H. Riddle, Chancellor of the University of Illinois at Chicago Circle, Dr. Gordon Misner, and Dr. Joseph Peterson also from the University of Illinois at Chicago, all provided both practical assistance and moral support. Ann Goolsby, of the University of California at Berkeley was kind enough to permit us to use the archives of the School of Criminology and to provide invaluable assistance relative to the "early days" of the field.

We are particularly indebted to the staff who worked many hours on the project, especially to Nancy Hirsch, Vicky Vasquez, and Julie Staszak. Ora Allen oversaw development of the manuscript as did Becky Rawa; many other individuals worked towards producing this final report of the project. We would also like to thank the members of the Joint Commission who were supportive, particularly during the developmental stages of the project, when disagreement and debates frequently occurred.

We are particularly indebted to Price Foster who had the vision and saw the need to better understand criminal justice higher education and to Jean Moore who served faithfully as project monitor over the years. Her foresight, patience, and contributions proved to be crucial to us. She was a friend but she was also an honest critic of the project who did not hesitate to set us back on course when we drifted.

Finally, we offer our sincere thanks to almost a hundred criminal justice educators who gathered in Chicago, Illinois on September 10-12, 1981 to discuss and criticize the prepublication draft of this report. Their assessment and recommendations had a tremendous influence. Many of the recommendations were welcome, and sections of chapters were revised to reflect the thoughts of these educational leaders. In many ways, this book is their final version of the project's report.

Like most research, ours is open to criticism. Many times we wished we could issue another questionnaire or another survey. Like most researchers, we feel that our results leave a great many questions unanswered and raise many new ones. We have developed a number of instruments that may be of value to researchers in the future; certainly the baseline data collected will be important in years to come. For the failures and omissions the authors take full responsibility, with the hope that the charity of our colleagues will allow them to understand the task we faced.

We hope that this book will set the stage for progress over the next decade. To those who were willing to help today so that there might be a future, we dedicate this book.

—Richard H. Ward
Project Director

Vincent J. Webb
Principal Investigator

QUEST FOR QUALITY

INTRODUCTION

The report of the Joint Commission on Criminology and Criminal Justice Education and Standards reflects in many ways the controversy surrounding criminal justice higher education. In the turbulent 1960's, an academic field of study was established that had virtually no body of literature, a relatively unprepared faculty, a tremendous influx of federal dollars, and a rapidly expanding student population whose administration was beyond the experience of most academics. The growth of criminal justice programs was nothing short of phenomenal. Some viewed them as tempory faddish programs that would not last in the academic world.

One outgrowth of the developmental period of the 1960's was an almost immediate inquiry by many educators and practitioners concerning the quality of criminal justice higher education, particularly when these programs gained visibility among academic offerings. In the 1970's, research and literature tended to corroborate deficiencies in criminal justice education, and as a result of the concern with quality, the Office of Criminal Justice Education and Training of the Law Enforcement Assistance Administration sponsored a project that led to the establishment of the Joint Commission.

Publication of the Commission's report represents the end of a long and sometimes tedious search for information and data that would support the development of minimum standards applicable to criminal justice higher education and to those programs that are labelled criminology but that in terms of curriculum might better be defined as criminal justice. Throughout the deliberations of the Commission, considerable disagreement occurred about the definitions of criminology and criminal justice. The Commission, however, had no real disagreement regarding what might be termed traditional criminology, and the majority agreed that a difference between criminology and criminal justice does exist.

Criminology has traditionally been a part of sociology in the United States. Practically all criminology programs exist within a larger sociology department and, at most, constitute only a portion of a student's overall sociological study. In addition, traditional criminology has emphasized the study of criminological theory and has paid much less attention to issues of public policy or criminal justice implementation.

The few programs existing outside of sociology departments but entitled criminology are usually more similar to the new criminal justice programs than to the traditional studies of sociology and criminology. In addition to stressing criminological theory and research, an equal or greater emphasis in these programs is placed on the education of criminal justice practitioners. Consequently, these programs of study share more in common with undergraduate and graduate criminal justice curricula than they share with traditional criminology programs.

To overcome some confusion and to bring greater uniformity to its work, the Joint Commission has concentrated its research efforts on programs labeled criminal justice or those that emphasize preparing students for careers in criminal justice. Some programs with the word criminology in their titles are included in the latter group. Consequently, the recommendations appearing in this volume apply to such programs and not to those undergraduate and graduate studies in criminology given in departments of sociology or emphasizing theory development and basic criminological research. As a matter of convenience, the educational programs discussed in this report, despite specific titles, will be referred to as criminal justice. Members of the Commission strongly agreed that minimum standards should be developed for *a field in transition that has not met with universal academic acceptance.*

During the course of its project the Commission agreed upon a broad-based plan that would provide a forum for a wide range

of opinions and thoughts that ultimately would be examined in
light of the findings of a large-scale research effort. The Commission sponsored a series of essays, research studies, and professional meetings, in which many of the findings in this
publication first emerged. The Commission also undertood its
own research, focusing primarily on administration, faculty,
and students in criminal justice.

In many ways the research effort might be viewed as being
overly ambitious. Much of the data collected could not be
generalized, and in many cases the volume of data was so large
as to prohibit its presentation in any one report. Although
these problems were not major, they did contribute to frustra-
tion among project staff who would have liked to have refined
the research further.

The Commission met many times during the course of the
project and played a significant role in its development. They
represented virtually all areas in criminology and criminal
justice and brought to discussions their unique backgrounds
covering a wide spectrum of experience and knowledge. Their
involvement was critical to the project's success.

As the research and the contributions of others began to
develop, it became apparent that one of the major deficiencies
of prior research into criminal justice higher education was the
lack of concern about the context within which criminal justice
has emerged during the past two decades. Much of the prior
research treated criminal justice education virtually in a
vacuum, with little consideration for events taking place in the
external world or for the academic environments within which
the field grew. If a broader context existed for the development of criminal justice education, it was related primarily to
the issue of crime control. Indeed, the term-"crime control program"-was commonly used throughout the early years of
federal funding for criminal justice education. Some thought
may have been given to the humanistic components of criminal
justice as a field in the earlier days, particularly regarding race
relations, but much of the early thinking must be viewed as
superficial at best.

Little or no consideration has been given to understanding
criminal justice programs either in their academic environment or in the larger society they are theoretically designed to
serve. Few comparisons have been made between the development of criminal justice and the development of traditional
academic disciplines. Much has been written about the so-
called "poor quality" of criminal justice students during the

past decade, yet little has been done to compare these students to those in other disciplines, particularly when many educators have complained about the declining quality of students.

Although discussion of criminal justice higher education within a broad context was not within the original scope of the project, the Commission felt that such an approach was important for several reasons: 1. A broader understanding of criminal justice will be useful in understanding the rationale behind many of the standards presented. 2. A broad effort is seen as providing a useful framework, heretofore missing for those who wish to continue studying criminal justice education. 3. Many criminal justice educators who are not of a traditional academic background are unfamiliar with various components of the academic world, just as many criminal justice educators who have only academic experience might be unfamiliar with components of the practitioner's experience. We hope that the broad parameters of this report will help to bridge some gaps in our knowledge and understanding.

The minimum standards presented here are just that--minimum standards. They in no way reflect all of the Commission's views of what standards are applicable within criminal justice. These standards are not permanent, nor are they meant to be, for the Commission members feel strongly that many standards will change over the next decade. They also realize that in exceptional situations the standards set forth here will not be applicable. Commission members recognize that standards must be reasonable if they are to be accepted by the field, and consequently, the greatest strength of the standards lies in the fact that they are supported by all members of the Commission.

The Commission did not take a position on the implementation of minimum standards. The Commission is convinced, however, that implementation is an issue that the field itself must consider. As a result, a chapter on various approaches to the implementation of standards, ranging from accreditation to self-evaluation, has been included in this report.

Most of the recommendations of the Joint Commission are not new; some have appeared in Pearson, et al.; Sherman; and the Academy of Criminal Justice Sciences' Accreditation Guidelines. Many of them have been proffered almost from the outset of criminal justice education. The discussion within each chapter of the report is designed to place a particular problem in perspective, to provide the arguments, both pro or con, to place the problem in a broad context, to provide the research findings when they exist, and to provide the rationale for the recommendations presented.

Criminal justice higher education not only has survived its early years but has recently prospered in terms of academic development and continued improvement of quality. This growth indicates that the criminal justice academic community is willing to change and is interested in improving the quality of programs, although no universal agreement as to the minimum standards for the field existed during its development.

If we are able to agree that minimum standards exist that are widely applicable and widely accepted, perhaps we can get on with the job of developing the field further. Faculty, administrators, and students must set the goals of the future. We hope these goals will go beyond the minimum standards recommended here. It is hoped that future researchers will draw upon the data of the Commission and further expand the information base. We now know much more about criminal justice education than we knew when the Commission's effort was begun, but the information only encourages us to learn more about criminal justice education in our quest for quality.

Chapter I

RECOMMENDATIONS

The Joint Commission's recommendations for criminal justice education are offered in the hope that they will be used in two different ways: 1. As standards, they can serve as a basis for comparison in assessing the quality of criminal justice educational efforts. 2. They can also serve as goals for use in the continued development of criminal justice education. Planning efforts, implementation strategies, and the evaluation of such efforts can draw on these recommendations for guidance.

The majority of the recommendations are not new; they are derived from earlier efforts. The recommendations of the National Advisory Commission on Higher Education for Police Officers and the Accreditation Guidelines developed by the Academy of Criminal Justice Sciences will be especially apparent. The revision, reaffirmation, or rejection of previous recommendations and standards as well as the development of new recommendations by the Joint Commission rest upon a broad approach that deserves some elaboration.

The Joint Commission developed a data base against which some of the previous recommendations and standards, both in criminal justice and similar fields, could be assessed. This data base was also used by the Commission as the major source of information in arriving at independent judgments about present levels of quality in criminal justice education. Consequently, the Commission, through its staff and subcontractors, amassed extensive data on the characteristics of criminal justice programs, students, and faculty.

In addition to the data base, the Commission's monograph series of commissioned empirical studies and scholarly essays on issues in criminal justice education was another important source developing the Commission's recommendations. These inquiries, which explored the basic nature of the field, the productivity and professionalism of its faculty, the status of criminal justice curricula, and the outcomes of doctoral education, produced insights and information used by the Commission in its deliberations.

The assessment of previously codified standards by a panel of experts was another major source of information used by the Commission in arriving at recommendations. Using a reputational technique, the Commission identified a panel of experts and asked them to assess over sixty standards that were taken from the report of the National Advisory Commission on Higher Education for Police Officers and the Accreditation Guidelines of the A.C.J.S. The degree of consensus among the panel of experts about the desirability of these recommendations and standards was instrumental in the Commission's decision-making. When consensus was extensive and expert opinion was not inconsistent with other Commission findings, the existing recommendation or standard received affirmation. When consensus was lacking, the Commission, through extensive deliberation, developed a modified or an alternative recommendation. The Commission found that extensive consensus existed for most recommendations and standards and was generally consistent with other Commission findings. Therefore, many of the recommendations are restatements of previously published recommendations.

Another important source of information used to develop a final set of recommendations resulted from a symposium sponsored by the Joint Commission. Almost a hundred criminal justice educators met in Chicago in September of 1981 to review and criticize a preliminary set of recommendations. Numerous comments and suggested revisions were made, and many of the suggestions have been accepted and incorporated in this report.

The recommendations that follow are based upon many sources of information used by the Joint Commission as it decided upon a final set of recommendations. A configuration of information derived from empirical studies, scholarly expositions, expert opinion, and months of deliberation underlies the recommendations, and the following chapters summarize this configuration. Although the Commission recognizes that its recommendations are changeable, the Commission believes that these recommendations can do much to accelerate the process of developing quality in criminal justice education.

The recommendations are based on the assumption that developing criminal justice education as a unified field is a desirable goal. Standards should have universal applicability, and a proposed set of standards should serve the goal of unification and not exacerbate the divisions that exist in the field. Therefore, the Joint Commission has, with only a few exceptions, avoided offering standards applicable only to two-year schools, four-year schools, or graduate institutions. The perceived and real differences among these different institutions are already too great. The Joint Commission recognizes these differences, especially between two-year and other institutions. However, the Commission believes that the standards that will best serve criminal justice education will be those that have the greatest applicability to all levels of criminal justice education.

ADMINISTRATION

A concern for parity and support for continued development of criminal justice education lies at the heart of the Joint Commission's recommendations relating to the administrative or organizational aspects of criminal justice education programs. As an established and legitimate field of academic study, criminal justice warrants a share of institutional resources commensurate with its contribution to the total educational effort of the institution. The institution, in acknowledging the legitimacy of criminal justice education, should provide such things as an identifiable program budget; a core of faculty; adequate educational support services; comprehensive learning resources, especially library services; and sufficient autonomy to enable the faculty and administration to engage in legitimate academic decision making, growth, and development. Institutions offering criminal justice education programs must also provide and support academic leadership for the program and the field. The program administrator is primarily a leader in a developing field of study, with broad responsibilities for the process of development.

For too long and in too many institutions of higher education, criminal justice, with its large student enrollments, has
been subject to exploitation. The use of criminal justice education to subsidize other academic and administrative programs
has severely hampered the field's development. The recommended standards that follow are aimed at assuring that a
foundation of resources exists for supporting the development
and dissemination of quality criminal justice education.

I.   The criminal justice program should be on a parity
         basis with all other academic units. If the program of
         study is a subdivision of a larger unit, it should retain
         sufficient autonomy to realize its objectives.

II.   At least one full-time faculty member or ad-
         ministrator should have the primary responsibility
         for the administration and direction of the criminal
         justice program.

III.   Funding allocations for the criminal justice program
         should be identifiable within the institution's budget.

IV.   Colleges and universities should offer a criminal
         justice education program only as a long-term com-
         mitment, demonstrated by institutional support com-
         mensurate with that provided to comparable pro-
         grams within the institution.

V.   Budgeting and funding should be provided at a level
         sufficient to maintain a quality educational program.
         The criminal justice program should not exist
         because of its ability to secure funding from sources
         external to the normal institutional budget processes.
         Institutions relying on outside funding for initiation
         and development of the criminal justice program
         must be prepared to fund the program fully within
         three years without relying on collateral sources of in-
         come.

VI.   The criminal justice faculty should actively par-
         ticipate in the preparation of their budget. The
         criminal justice administrator's role should carry as
         much authority as the role of administrators of other
         units similarly organized within the institution. The

criminal justice administrator should be recognized
as the primary leader in criminal justice education at
the institutional level.

VII.   An institution with a criminal justice program should
provide resources for a criminal justice library collection. Formal, written arrangements with other
criminal justice libraries readily accessible to
students and faculty may be considered in partial
compliance with this requirement.

VIII.   The content of criminal justice library resources and
the level of funding should be proportionate to the
resources and levels of funding of other academic
units. Allocation of library resources should reflect
appropriate emphasis on acquisition of historical,
contemporary, and periodical holdings in relation to
the criminal justice curricular objectives. Substantially more extensive library holdings are required for
graduate and research programs.

IX.   College libraries should engage in retroactive acquisition programs to bring library resources for criminal
justice education to the present levels of other programs in the college.

X.   The criminal justice faculty should actively participate in the selection of library materials.

XI.   The accessibility of learning resources should be commensurate with student and faculty needs.

XII.   Adequate space, supplies, and equipment should be
provided for classes, laboratories, and offices for
faculty and staff. Adequate secretarial, clerical, and
other supportive staff assistance should be provided.
The supportive resources provided to the criminal
justice program should be no less than those provided
to other academic units.

XIII.   Criminal justice officials and other members of
criminal justice education program advisory boards
should avoid direct participation in such academic
decisions as faculty selection or promotion and curriculum content.

XIV.   College administrators should strengthen criminal
        justice education as a force for change, especially by
        protecting criminal justice education programs from
        pressures of local agencies.

CURRICULA

The Joint Commission's recommended standards for curricula are primarily concerned with fostering criminal justice
education programs oriented toward the intellectual development of the complete individual. The goal of criminal justice
education should be to increase the general level of understanding of the problems of crime and criminal justice. The out-
come of a criminal justice education should be individuals who
have a comprehensive understanding of crime, the criminal
justice system, and the broader social context in which these
exist. These individuals will have an ample exposure to the
physical and life sciences, the humanities, and the social
sciences. They will also have substantial exposure to course
work that focuses on developing logical, analytical, and conceptual skills. Exposure to different cultures, values, and
ideologies are essential ingredients of quality criminal justice
education. This same education must also be systematic and
interdisciplinary, and criminal justice programs should emphasize these characteristics. Responsible criminal justice
education will strive to provide a rigorous yet flexible learning
experience so that students may achieve a foundation for
meeting a lifetime of challenges. This experience serves as the
premise for the following recommended standards.

I.   The basic purpose of criminal justice education is to
        develop educated citizens who have a comprehensive
        understanding of the problems of crime and the
        criminal justice system. This purpose must be
        reflected throughout the criminal justice curricula.

II.   Criminal justice curricula should recognize the inter-
        disciplinary nature of the field.

III.   All college programs focusing on criminal justice
        should provide a broad education, useful to many
        service-giving careers during the future.

IV.   Criminal justice curricula should recognize the interdependence of cultural norms, traditions, value systems, and social responses to problem solving.

V.   The criminal justice program should provide for the study and analysis of social goals and their relationships to governmental policies.

VI.   Criminal justice education programs using a criminal justice system framework for their required curricula should include comprehensive treatment of the broad social and political system which serves as the context for criminal justice.

VII.   Every criminal justice education program should include required courses in the ethics of working in the criminal justice system.

VIII.   Provisions should be made to encourage criminal justice students to take a wide variety of elective courses.

IX.   Criminal justice curricula should reflect the institution's goals through its own specific program goals and statements of purpose.

X.   Once a logic or rationale is developed for a criminal justice program, it should be adhered to when designing and reviewing curriculum features.

XI.   Criminal justice programs should be oriented toward the intellectual development of the whole person. Basic agency skill training and course work which is not designed to develop logical, analytical, or cognitive skills or to develop the reasoning capabilities of the student are clearly not a part of the goal of an academic degree program.

XII.   Criminal justice programs should replace vocational training courses or courses that train students to perform specific tasks, with analytical and conceptual courses on issues related to those tasks.

XIII.   Credit for life experience in the criminal justice field should be awarded only after careful review, and when it is consistent with the guidelines recommended by the American Council on Education and endorsed by the Council on Post-secondary Accreditation. It should also be awarded only if the life experience meets program requirements and is consistent with the general crediting regulations of the college or university.

XIV.   Colleges should grant no academic credit for attendance at criminal justice agency training programs.

XV.   To insure a balanced program within the interdisciplinary field of criminal justice, overspecialization should be avoided at the undergraduate level.

XVI.   The required number of specialized courses in criminal justice at the two-year and four-year undergraduate levels should not exceed one fourth of the total course work for the degree.

XVII.   To insure a high level of quality in the curriculum and in instruction, institutions should review and evaluate their programs at least every three years. This review should involve students, faculty, and outside experts.

XVIII.   College courses on criminal justice should be continually revised to reflect and incorporate rapidly growing research findings.

XIX.   Undergraduate students should be exposed to a program that includes the study of research methods, statistics, and computer science.

FACULTY

The recommended standards on faculty generally reflect four related concerns: qualifications, utilization, development, and workload. A special concern for increasing the number of racial and ethnic minorities and women in criminal justice faculty is also reflected in the following standards.

The Commission's recommendations on faculty qualifications reflect an increasing emphasis and reliance on educational preparation and academic credentials in decisions regarding faculty hiring. Practical agency experience should not be
penalized nor should it be substituted for academic preparation and credentials. Criminal justice education, like other
fields concerned with social and policy problems, relies on
various forms of vicarious learning in its knowledge development and pedagogy. The Joint Commission recognizes the
legitimate role and use of part-time faculty in staffing criminal
justice programs. However, the Commission strongly recom-
mends that the use of part-time faculty be kept to a minimum;
that the qualifications of part-time faculty be generally the
same as for full-time faculty; and that the decision to use part-
time faculty be based on an academic rather than a cost effective rationale.

Improving criminal justice education means improving
criminal justice faculty. All faculty should have ample opportunity for professional development, and they should be expected to take advantage of opportunities to develop
themselves.

Future increases in the quality of criminal justice education
will also be determined by the field's ability to expand its
limited knowledge base. In the Joint Commission's view,
criminal justice education can now be characterized as a
teaching field. Too few faculty and programs have placed an
adequate emphasis on research. Research is the primary
means by which the field can develop its body of knowledge.
The lack of emphasis on research in the past has made the expansion of knowledge on crime and criminal justice very difficult. In the future, research should be an expected activity
for all criminal justice faculty.

Crime and the criminal justice system have been and continue to be special problems for America's minorities. A
responsible criminal justice education must be sensitive to the
concerns of minorities, and this sensitivity should be made apparent throughout the field. Although immediate steps must
be taken to increase the number of racial and ethnic minorities
and women in the criminal justice faculty, it is also necessary
to develop a long-term strategy to increase the pool of minority
and female graduate students from which future faculty will be
drawn.

Criminal justice education, its basic nature, its future direction, and its future level of quality depends on the faculty in

the field. The following recommended standards for faculty are designed to make sure that the best possible faculty are available to fulfill the responsibility of providing criminal justice education.

I. Educational background, teaching ability, research, and commitment should be the most important criteria of faculty selection in criminal justice education programs. Prior criminal justice employment, although recognized as a potential asset, should not be a requirement for faculty selection.

II. Faculty should demonstrate an aptitude for teaching and possess research competence as evidenced by academic preparation, publications, and involvement in significant regional or national professional activities.

III. Minimum academic qualifications for teaching full time in associate degree programs should include a law degree or a master's degree with concentration in a content area relating to or complementing the area of instruction. Degrees should be from institutions holding national or regional accreditation.

IV. Minimum academic qualifications for faculty teaching in baccalaureate and graduate programs normally should include a doctorate degree with concentration in a content area relating to or complementing the area of instruction. Exceptions may be made when other terminal degrees are more appropriate to specific teaching and research needs. Justifications for exceptions should rest with the institution.

V. Colleges and universities should provide a program of continuous support for faculty development.
    a. This program should include opportunities for faculty growth and development in teaching, community service, and especially research in criminal justice.
    b. Expanded opportunities should be provided for the improvement and development of teaching skills.
    c. A continuous evaluation of faculty performance

should occur, focusing on and promoting excellence in teaching, research, publications, and service to the institution and to the public.

VI.   Colleges and universities should rely on a core of full-time faculty to staff their criminal justice education programs. Part-time faculty should not be employed for more than 25 percent of the total annual credit hours offered by the institution.

VII.   The nature of this field of study, which involves the application of knowledge to a specific type and set of social problems, creates a unique role for part-time, adjunct faculty, and their appointment often enriches program offerings.
       a. Generally, the academic qualifications of part-time faculty should be the same as those for full-time faculty members.
       b. Part-time faculty should be appointed for academic reasons, not to effect institutional cost savings.
       c. Part-time faculty should not constitute the integral core of the faculty, nor should they be viewed by students or by the institution as the primary criminal justice faculty of the institution.

VIII. Criminal justice undergraduate and graduate students should receive no more than 25 percent of their criminal justice course work from part-time instructors. No more than one-third of the total credit hours in criminal justice should be offered by the same instructor.

IX.   Criminal justice professional organizations and institutions with criminal justice education programs should initiate and support affirmative action programs in attracting women and minorities as faculty and as students at both undergraduate and graduate levels.

X.   Because graduate programs have an important function in providing a supply of new faculty, these programs have a unique responsibility to recruit competent female and minority students. In turn, female and ethnic minority students enrolled in undergraduate criminal justice education programs need appropriate faculty role models.

XI.   Institutions that offer criminal justice education programs should give explicit recognition to the research needs of the field. Research should be viewed as a faculty activity equal in importance to teaching.

XII.   Depending upon whether a faculty member is in a two-year, baccalaureate, or graduate program, the responsibility for engaging in different types of research activity will vary. At two-year institutions, "research" will typically involve the consumption of the research findings of others for use in the presentation of materials for class instruction. At four-year and graduate institutions, faculty members should be actually conducting research.

     a.   Time for research should be clearly defined as part of the faculty work load.

     b.   Research credentials should be emphasized in decisions to hire, promote, and grant tenure to faculty.

     c.   Many institutions consciously or unconsciously erect impediments to research, and these should be recognized in the periodic evaluations of faculty.

     d.   Doctoral education in criminal justice should emphasize the development of research skills.

STUDENTS

In comparison to administration, curricula, and faculty, the Commission offers few recommendations on students. Students are the raison d'etre for criminal justice education, and in its deliberations, the Commission assumed that all faculty and administrators, in criminal justice education want the best possible criminal justice education for their students. That education must be characterized by the highest possible level of quality. The preceding recommendations on administration, curricula, and faculty were reaffirmed or designed for the purpose of providing that education in the interest of criminal justice students.

Based upon the research conducted by and for the Joint Commission as well as the thoughtful commentary provided by leaders in the field, the Commission decided to offer recommendations that are based upon and highlight the observation that criminal justice students are really no different from other college students. College and university faculty, staff, and administrators should hold the same set of expectations for criminal justice students as they do for other students. Admission criteria, examination procedures, grading criteria, assignments, and participation in collegiate life should be the same for criminal justice students as for other students. Criminal justice students should be provided the same level and quality of educational support provided to other college students. Quality support services like academic advising and career counseling should be available to all students, regardless of major.

Criminal justice education probably offers students a disservice by claiming that they differ from the general college population. Differences that may have existed in the past have become minimal. Support for claims of difference is hard to maintain, and criminal justice education in the future must be based on educating students representative of the general college and university population. The recommended standards that follow reflect general representative education.

I.   Colleges, universities, and criminal justice programs should treat criminal justice students and non-criminal justice students equally. Exceptions, favorable or unfavorable, for criminal justice students are inappropriate and unnecessary. Admissions policies, student performance expectations, assignments, evaluation and grading, and learning environment should be the same for both criminal justice and non-criminal justice students.

     a.   All full-time and part-time students should be provided with basic services such as programs of orientation, academic advisement, counseling, and guidance.

     b.   All full-time and part-time students should be provided with career counseling that provides accurate information on job opportunities and entry level requirements and restrictions.

     c.   Colleges and universities should attempt to involve as fully as possible all full-time and part-time students in activities that comprise collegiate life.

Chapter II

HISTORICAL DEVELOPMENT OF CRIMINOLOGY AND CRIMINAL JUSTICE

The study of crime and crime related issues did not begin with the development of criminal justice education programs; the roots of scholarly interest in crime may be traced to a much earlier time. Those familiar with the works of the pioneers of what came to be known as "criminology" should recognize both the contributions of those pioneers as well as the foundation they laid for the field's future. Much of the early American criminological literature was written by European authors (Simpson, 1979, p. 43). The development of criminology in the United States can be traced to a time before the turn of the century. Many of the writings that appeared then and in the early 1900's probably set the tone for the field of sociological criminology.

At the turn of the century apparently little disagreement took place about either the definition of criminology or its academic place in sociology departments, probably due to the broadening nature of sociology during the early 1900's. During this period the study of criminology at the undergraduate level generally involved one or more courses in the curriculum as part of a broad sociological emphasis. Furthermore a great emphasis was placed on research and research problems within the developing discipline.

Much of the sociological literature of the 1950's focused on the development and critique of theories related to crime and juvenile delinquency. Many of these works became the literature for the development of criminal justice programs.

Within the field of criminology several differing philosophies exist that may have contributed to what Simpson (1979, p.42) terms "a crisis of identity." Several authors commissioned by the Joint Commission (Myren and Conrad, 1979; Zalman, 1981; Morn, 1980) have offered different explanations of what criminology is, what it should be, and how it differs from criminal justice. In a critique of these publications, C. Ray Jeffery (Joint Commission Correspondence, 1981) attempted to place in perspective the problem of integrating criminology and criminal justice.

> All of the papers (Conrad, Myren, Morn, and Zalman) agree that criminology is an academic pursuit related to the behavioral sciences, sociology primarily but also psychology, biology, anthropology, political science, and economics. Conrad places emphasis on criminology as a behavioral science, and criminal justice as the application of knowledge. Myren rejects criminology as a basis for criminal justice since it is too dependent on sociology and is too narrow in scope. He includes criminology within criminal justice, and then he incorporates criminal justice in a broader field of justiciology. Morn finds in the history of criminology and criminal justice basic unresolved conflicts. A.S.C. grew out of the National Association of College Police Training Officials, under the leadership of August Vollmer. A.S.C. developed later a more behavioral science orientation, and as a result in 1963 the more applied members of the American Society of Criminology (A.S.C.) split off to form the International Association of Police Professors, which became the Academy of Criminal Justice Sciences in 1970. Thus A.S.C. started from a criminal justice group, became criminology, and then emerged as A.S.C. and A.C.J.S. by 1970.
>
> From the standpoint of professional affiliation, there is no such thing as "a criminologist" or a "criminology program." We have sociologists or psychologists or economists who take an interest in crime and criminal behavior and they may designate themselves as criminologists, but there is no well-recognized academic discipline called criminology as

there is for sociology, psychology, and biology. The recent emergence of criminal justice programs has further blurred the distinction between criminology and criminal justice. The fact that many criminal justice programs include criminology, and that some criminologists concern themselves with research in areas of the police, courts, and corrections further blurs the distinction.

Zalman states that criminology and criminal justice differ, that criminology is devoted to research whereas criminal justice is devoted to practice, that they overlap in interests and pursuits, and that neither is a science or discipline. Zalman views criminology and criminal justice as interdisciplinary fields that rest on basic social sciences. However, Zalman (p.35) makes a comparison between criminology and medicine which is confusing to say the least. He notes that medicine is applied basic biological science, whereas in criminology the practitioners are scientists. He goes on to state that in criminology a distinction between researchers and practitioners is not applicable since very little criminological knowledge has been applied. He notes that practitioners are scientists and the field is not a science. It is hard to understand how people can practice something which in itself is not a science. I would argue that medicine is an applied field allied with the biological and behavioral sciences. Using such an analogy criminology would be the behavioral science foundation upon which the application of knowledge is made in the real world of criminal justice. Criminal justice is thus like engineering or medicine or law, a professional grouping bent on the application of knowledge.

This analogy breaks down, however. Because criminal justice is related to and controlled by lawyers and the law profession, the behavioral sciences have not been allowed to develop alternative approaches to crime control. The ideas of the Positive School were tacked onto the criminal justice system. We refer to this with the euphemism of "corrections" though we understand that this is falsehood and deception. If we were serious about treatment and rehabilitation, we would have divorced it from the prison system a long time ago.

This introduces a basic issue not discussed so far by those who are involved in these discussions. There exists a basic conflict between criminology and criminal justice that has not been overcome and this conflict is found in the history of criminology as presented by Morn and others. Criminal justice is committed to a policy orientation based on physical force, violence, punishment, and prisons. The end result of the criminal justice process is prison or execution. The justification of the system is retribution and deterrence, and policy is based on this philosophy of law irrespective of the social and personal consequences. The lawyer places great emphasis upon legal procedures for determining that a crime has been committed, that the person charged is guilty of the crime, and that all of the formal procedures have been carried out. By these means the role of the law is preserved in the determination of guilt and the disposition of the crime problem, but it does nothing to enhance our understanding of crime or criminals.

Criminology must take its share of the blame for not developing a more scientific view of behavior than it has. Myren is correct in castigating criminologists for their lack of success, but he is not correct in turning the system over to policy makers or justicians. Myren cites Radzinowicz in his discussion of why criminal justice should predominate over criminology. However, the spirit of Radzinowicz's statement is misunderstood by Myren. Radzinowicz was arguing for the need for the establishment of a center for the study of criminology as an interdisciplinary science, and he included in this definition the study of those measures taken to prevent and control crime. These studies, according to his statement, quoted Myren, constitute criminology. Radzinowicz was talking about a West Point for the study of crime, not a legal bureaucracy which carried on traditions of hundreds of years ago. This is a far cry from the system of justice as we now practice it which is dominated by policy-makers -- politicians and lawyers -- and which has little if any use for basic behavioral research.

This conflict is nowhere better illustrated than in the recent attempts to create a justice model of crime by such policy/law-oriented people as Wilson, van den Haag, Ehrlich, Fogel, Morris, and Hawkins (see Morn, p.18, for discussion). In these discussions prisons punishment, and executions are justified as fitting within a justice model of the criminal justice system. Here is a real rejection of criminology as it has been known within academic circles.

We must conclude, therefore that there is no basic support either within the academic or within the political system for the development of a science of criminology. Criminology has in recent years made a living by attaching itself to L.E.A.A. programs in the furtherance of the law and order model of criminal justice. The issue remains as to what sort of support must be given to the development of criminology as an honest academic discipline comparable to sociology, psychology, and biology. We now see criminology as an aspect of sociology or psychology or social work or law or public administration, or even worse, as an aspect of vocationalism which furnishes bodies for the criminal justice systems.

Those who have a background in criminal justice --lawyers, police, correctional officials, court personnel--have a different view of crime and justice from those with a background in the behavioral sciences. Lawyers and police are either not interested in behavioral research or support a move to do away with behavioral research. Scientists are critical of attempts to build more prisons, to execute more criminals, and to create larger police departments in order to curb the growing crime rate. Given these assumptions there is no meeting ground or commonality for criminology and criminal justice. We must either find a new approach to crime control or we must be resigned to accept the basic conflict between classicism and positivism for many years to come.

Undoubtedly, some might want to disagree with Dr.

Jeffery's conclusions. Perhaps the development of criminal justice has helped to broaden criminology so that research questions about the criminal justice system, and not just criminal behavior, are now legitimate criminological fare. Perhaps the issue is academic, because the members of the Joint Commission agreed that a field of study identifiable as "criminal justice" exists. Criminology played an important role in the development of criminal justice as a separate field of study within academe, and much of the work of criminologists serves as literature for an emerging field.

THE EMERGENCE OF CRIMINAL JUSTICE

Criminal justice as a unique academic discipline in American higher education is generally viewed as having its roots in the development of August Vollmer's police school at the University of California at Berkeley in 1916 (Carte, 1975). Vollmer's efforts to establish a curriculum in criminal justice were made during at least twenty years, and he was successful in establishing a course of study that may be viewed as the forerunner of today's criminal justice programs.

Between the late 1920's and the end of the 1930's, a number of prestigious academic institutions established separate programs of study for criminal justice professionals, primarily the police. These institutions included the University of Chicago, the University of California, Indiana University, Michigan State University, San Jose State University, and the University of Washington (Simpson, 1979, p.50).

In these programs criminal justice courses tended to address administrative matters, whereas criminology courses generally centered on the study of crime and delinquency from a sociological perspective.

During the period between 1930 and 1950, emphasis was placed on the education of police, and most of this education was provided at the community college or two-year level. Several programs in corrections existed at the four-year and graduate level, and most of those programs appear to have been given in departments of sociology (German, 1957; Karacki and Galvin, 1968; Foster, 1974; Simpson, 1979). The nature of the students enrolled in these programs differed. The law enforcement programs were likely to enroll in-service students, whereas the corrections programs enrolled a higher percentage of pre-service students, most of whom were interested in careers in probation or parole rather than in corrections.

The end of World War II brought about another major impetus for growth in criminal justice when law enforcement agencies began to emphasize training. California, generally through the efforts of Vollmer, began to establish minimum entrance and training standards, consequently creating a need for higher education. Again, most of the higher education programs were implemented at the two-year community college level (Stephens, 1976).

The period between 1950 and 1960 was characterized by increasing changes in the entire criminal justice system, although most changes were occurring in relatively few cities and states. California and New York took the lead in establishing formal training programs, with the implementation of P.O.S.T. (Police Officers Standards and Training) in California in 1960 (Stephens, 1976). With these changes came a growing number of collegiate level programs. By 1965 approximately sixty-five criminal justice related programs were in existence (Foster, 1974; Pelfrey, 1978). In some measure these programs grew due to the number of returning veterans from the Korean War, many of whom exercised G.I. Bill benefits to pursue higher education in areas related to criminal justice. Parole and probation officers usually received their degrees from schools of social work (Simpson, 1979, p.53), but a trend toward specific studies in corrections and sociology was evident. During this period few pre-service law enforcement students were enrolled, and the emphasis in many of the two-year programs was on training courses rather than on philosophical and research-related issues. An exception was San Jose State University where, according to Misner, about 90 percent of the six hundred students were pre-service. (Misner, personal correspondence)

The major change in criminal justice education occurred due to the involvement of the federal government in the late 1960's when several major governmental commissions identified deficiencies within the criminal justice system. These committees included the McCone Commission, which investigated the 1965 Watts riots; the Kerner Commission, which undertook an investigation of civil disorders, the Walker Commission, which investigated the causes of preventing violence; and the President's Commission on Law Enforcement and Administration of Justice (1967), which addressed numerous issues related to criminal justice. All of these reports had one common theme-- the need to improve the quality of criminal justice personnel, particularly the police. Although training was viewed as an important goal, a strong belief existed that the future of a "professional" criminal justice system had to be based upon higher educational requirements for its members. Simpson (1979) noted that an important premise of virtually all recommendations during this period was a commitment to a criminal justice system that could be characterized as having a service approach with less emphasis on the quasi-military nature of the system, particularly in law enforcement. Most early supporters of higher education for criminal justice personnel believed that exposure to education would "liberalize" the system, providing broader exposure to wordly views. As Simpson stated:

> The reasons generally advanced in support of the recommendations of the various federal commissions regarding mandatory higher education for criminal justice personnel can be grouped conveniently into two categories: those that support this level of education by assuming the benefit of it as a generally liberalizing influence on police agencies and those that suggest that it has specific, and identifiable, effects on job performance. (p.56) (See also Sterling, 1974; Berkley, 1969; Bressler, 1967.)

If the late 1960's served as a turning point in the history of criminal justice, those years also served as a turning point in the history of the nation due to an unpopular war in Vietnam, domestic disturbances in the inner cities, and unrest on University campuses.

During the 1970's, higher education faced a series of challenges that continue to be debated. Howard R. Bowen, (1980), who has conducted extensive research of higher education, maintains that performance of the system is perceived as having deteriorated in six ways: shorter academic schedules, an increase in the size of institutions, less effective faculties, difficulties in addressing the needs of disadvantaged students, excessive student vocational interests, and emphasis on the marketing of institutions.

Whatever the reasons, most educational institutions underwent a series of changes during the 1960's and 1970's. Some argue that student dissent had a favorable impact on institutions (Mayhew, 1972). Others believe that most of the problems of American education were due to external forces, such as legal intervention, collective bargaining, and the involvement of special interest groups (Wood, 1980). Changes were occurring during a period in which criminal justice programs were being implemented almost daily and into which the federal government was spending millions of dollars for both education and research through the newly established Law Enforcement Assistance Administration (L.E.A.A.). Some financially hard-pressed institutions viewed federal funding with sighs of relief. Others felt that criminal justice was being used to attract students who would take some courses in the social sciences and humanities.

By 1973 approximately 700 programs in the field had been established and by 1978 more than 1,200 programs existed (Foster, 1974; Pearson, 1978). Research conducted by the Joint Commission identified approximately fifteen hundred institutions which offered at least some course of study in criminology or criminal justice. The rapid proliferation of programs made planning, coordinating, and staffing the field of study in a systematic manner difficult, if not impossible. Furthermore, many of these programs were implemented on college campuses without the traditional academic procedures for review and appraisal, or they were hastily established through the appropriate procedures. Much of the early criticism of criminal justice programs can be traced to these years when the number of qualified faculty was inadequate, very little agreement existed as to the philosophical base of the programs or the curricula, and institutional resources were usually inadequate to provide courses of study. However, because most students and many of the faculty in these programs were part-time, little or no protest arose. Indeed, many faculty and students in criminal justice saw being affiliated with higher education as a significant achievement and did not want to jeopardize that achievement.

In 1973 the National Advisory Commission on Criminal Justice Standards and Goals reaffirmed the view that higher education was critical to the development of criminal justice, recommending that all police officers should have a baccalaureate degree by the year 1982 (U.S. National Advisory Commission, 1973, p.311). This report created further efforts to develop criminal justice education, and backed by federal funds, law enforcement educators and administrators pushed to establish an increasing number of programs. The implementation of criminal justice education may be contrasted with the remarks of many leading educators who were decrying the decline of higher education. Clark Kerr, in a 1978 article entitled "Higher Education: Paradise Lost," perhaps summed up the views of many educators who felt that the transition from an elite to a mass access to universal education was damaging higher education. He warned that higher education was increasingly coming under political and external social controls which were hampering academe.

By the early 1970's the Law Enforcement Education Program (L.E.E.P.) established by the Omnibus Crime Control and Safe Streets Act of 1968 (Public Law 90-351) was functioning. L.E.E.P. was administered by the Law Enforcement Assistance Administration (L.E.A.A.). The Program evolved from the rhetoric of a Great Society view of federal involvement in social change as the result of legislation written in the wake of summer urban violence and racial discontent. The first federal funds were mailed to 485 colleges and universities to use as student grants and loans beginning in January, 1969. In its first six months, L.E.E.P. assisted 17,992 students, ninety four percent of whom were in- service officers. The program appropriation of $6.5 million for these first six months was nearly tripled to $18 million during the next year.

Table II-1 provides an historical summary of the activity of L.E.E.P. from its founding in fiscal 1969 to its last, moribund season in 1980. From a peak season in 1975, when $40 million was appropriated for more than 113,000 students at more than a hundred schools, L.E.E.P. steadily declined in influence. The decline may be attributed to the shifting standards of the Program directors and to a federal government rapidly losing interest in educational funding for state, local, and private agencies.

Perhaps the most controversial of L.E.E.P.'s stated purposes was its attempt to influence curriculum planners. L.E.A.A. recognized that much of L.E.E.P.'s money was being paid to in-service individuals in police science programs oriented to teaching skills rather than to college majors in academic programs of criminal justice. To assure that Program administrators distinguished between training and degree-credit programs, the 1969 federal program guidelines stipulated that Program funds could not be used for training

TABLE II-1
L.E.E.P. ACTIVITY 1969-1980

Fiscal Year	Academic Year	Appropriation (Thousands)	Number of Schools	Number of Students
1969	6 mos of 1968-69	$ 6,500	485	17,992
1970	1969-70	18,000	735	51,358
1971	1970-71	21,250	890	64,836
1972	1971-72	29,250	962	81,165
1973	1972-73	40,000	993	102,147
1974	1973-74	40,000	1,036	113,119
1975	1974-75	40,000	1,065	109,310
1976	1975-76	40,000	1,031	84,458
1976 Transition Budget				
1977	1976-77	40,000	1,012	79,203
1978	1977-78	40,000	994	72,250
1979	1978-79	30,000	955	65,865
1980	1979-80	25,000	867	31,692
1980*	1980-81	-0-	830	22,500

*Student participation not final. This is an estimate.

Source: Office of Criminal Justice
Education and Training. L.E.A.A.

**TABLE II-2
L.E.E.P. RECIPIENTS
1968-1981**

Year	In-service Total Number of Students	Percentage of Total
1968-69 (6 mos.)	17,992	94.00
1969-70	51,358	85.56
1970-71	64,836	81.83
1971-72	81,165	80.96
1972-73	102,147	83.09
1973-74	113,119	89.84
1974-75	109,310	89.00
1975-76	84,458	91.80
1976-77	79,203	93.29
1977-78	72,250	92.85
1978-79	65,865	94.0
1979-80	31,692	94.0
1980-81*	22,500	95.0

*Final student participation figures not available. This is an estimate.

Source: Office of Criminal Justice Education and Training. L.E.A.A.

and that schools, at a minimum, must offer fifteen semester (or equivalent) credit hours in courses *directly related* to law enforcement in order to qualify to make student loans. Consequently, the Program attempted to change the nature of curricula at individual institutions by threatening to withhold funds unless criteria were met.

The Omnibus Crime Control Act of 1970 provided new authority for L.E.E.P. to support planning and development of curricula, teaching materials, and faculty, and research related to such efforts. This authority of the 1970 Act was incorporated without change into the Crime Control Act of 1973 as Part D, Section 406 (e). This authority resulted from L.E.A.A.'s concern over the nature of criminal justice degree programs and recognized a need to offset the training orientation of two-year schools and to provide the four-year faculties with more experience.

Eventually, beginning in 1976-77, L.E.A.A. used this Program authority to mount projects designed to improve the quality of higher education related to crime and to improve the capability of criminal justice agencies to assess and project their manpower needs, including the needs for the training and education of personnel. L.E.A.A., as a result, initiated research on the impact of education on police attitudes and performance, the development of a model for designing curricula in response to criminal justice system needs, and the initiation of this study of minimum standards by the Joint Commission.

By the late 1970's, the numbers of L.E.E.P.-supported students were declining and the proportion of L.E.E.P.-supported individuals within criminal justice programs was decreasing. By 1980, the time of the Joint Commission's survey, only 24 percent of the students enrolled in criminal justice courses were being funded by L.E.E.P. This percentage includes those students receiving partial funding from the Programs; see Chapter VIII. Finally, the federal government itself created the bureaucratic scenario for L.E.E.P.'s demise. In 1979, the Justice System Improvement Act provided for the transfer of Program administration from the U.S. Department of Justice to the new Department of Education. In 1981, the Department of Education, its own days numbered in the Reagan Administration, began officially to end the Law Enforcement Education Program.

In addition to being eligible for L.E.E.P., many veterans of the Korean and Vietnam Wars were also eligible to receive G.I. Bill benefits. For many police officers this eligibility for funds proved to be an opportunity to attend school and to be paid an amount that was frequently equivalent to that earned in a part- time job. The influx of in-service students with veterans' benefits into the educational scene further complicated development of criminal justice; a great many students took advantage of the opportunity to increase their income although it is difficult to estimate how many were serious about education. Determining how many in-service students began their education only to discontinue it when their veteran's benefits ended is impossible. Some critics argue that the number is high, whereas supporters maintain there is no higher than the 50 percent attrition common in higher education.

During the middle of the 1970's the majority of criminal justice students were in-service police. Subsequent critics of criminal justice development maintained that the quality of the students in these programs was generally low, although relatively little evidence exists to support their view. Nevertheless, the criticism prevailed when pre-service students entered criminal justice studies in the late 1970's. During this period continuing criticism occurred within higher education about the general quality of students (see Abel, 1978; Chase, 1978; Winthrop, 1978). Concern was also growing about measuring the quality of students in a manner that excluded racial, religious, or ethnic considerations (Healy, 1977).

Some viewed the establishment of criminal justice programs as a phenomenon which would pass and which had no permanency in the academic world. Many people assumed that either the population of in-service students would eventually decline or that federal funding would be reduced; either event would end most programs. Others with a different vision recognized the interest of many pre-service students in criminal justice education and predicted change and growth. Toward the end of the 1970's criminal justice programs underwent another difficult transition from educating mostly part-time students to a student body that was full-time and more traditional.

Within the educational community, criminal justice programs were established and organized in different ways. Some were housed in conjunction with other academic departments like sociology. Some were viewed as programs which were something less than recognized departments; others achieved independent departmental status; many were given an amorphous status. Some were housed in colleges of liberal arts and sciences and others in vocational or professional colleges.

Faculty during the 1960's apparently were recruited from the field of practice. Many of them had little or no familiarity with the academic process. Most were appointed as adjunct or part-time faculty. A significant percentage did not hold doctorates or traditionally valued academic credentials; few had publication records, and fewer had valid research experience. Consequently, from the beginning, criminal justice faculty were viewed by their colleagues as being "different." Because many came from military or quasi-military occupations, they were often unfamiliar with the "community of scholars" approach to problem-solving. On most campuses the power of the faculty rested in the social behavioral sciences, fields in which many faculty were less than enamored of the criminal justice system. On many campuses feelings of hostility developed between students and faculty in criminal justice and those in other disciplines. As a result, problems of acceptance occurred within the academic community.

Conflict also occurred among educators, particularly about the direction criminal justice should take. In 1963 a group of educators resigned from the American Society of Criminology to form the International Association of Police Professors (I.A.P.P.). The group viewed themselves as applied criminologists, as contrasted to "sociological criminologists" (Morn, 1980, pp.12-13). In 1970, the membership of I.A.P.P. voted to change the name of the Association to the Academy of Criminal Justice Sciences (A.C.J.S.) to represent the majority of educators in criminology and criminal justice education, although many educators hold membership in both A.S.C. and A.C.J.S. Other professional associations also maintain an interest in the field, either through members who are educators or pratitioners. Some of these include the American Sociological Association, the American Society for Public Administration, the American Academy for Professional Law Enforcement, the International Association of Chiefs of Police, the American Correctional Association, the American Psychological Association, and the Society for Study of Social Problems.

GRADUATE STUDY IN CRIMINAL JUSTICE

Graduate study was not one of the Joint Commission's primary areas of investigation, although some parallels between undergraduate and graduate program development dur-

TABLE II-3
ADJUSTED RANK ORDER OF MEAN PRESTIGE SCORES OF
GRADUATE PROGRAMS IN CRIMINOLOGY-CRIMINAL JUSTICE

Rank	School	Total Sample	ASC Sample	ACJS Sample
1.	John Jay College of Criminal Justice	4.636	4.533	4.857
2.	State Univ. of New York at Albany	4.511	4.649	4.214
3.	Florida State	4.363	4.133	4.857
4.	Michigan State	4.102	3.849	4.643
5.	Univ. of Pennsylvania	3.602	3.799	3.178
6.	Rutgers University	3.420	3.416	3.428
7.	Sam Houston State	3.409	3.099	4.071
8.	University of Maryland	3.102	3.183	2.929
9.	The American University	3.067	2.916	3.393
10.	Pennsylvania State	2.909	2.833	3.071
11.	San Jose State	2.772	2.616	3.107
12.	Southern Illinois	2.715	2.433	3.322
13.	Washington State	2.318	2.350	2.250
14.	Arizona State	2.284	2.149	2.571
15.	Temple University	2.102	1.800	2.750
16.	University of Louisville	2.068	1.650	2.964
17.	Eastern Kentucky	2.022	1.633	2.857
18.	Indiana State	2.011	1.733	2.607
19.	California State-Long Beach	1.897	1.733	2.250
20.	University of Alabama-Birmingham	1.829	1.466	2.607
21.	Virginia Commonwealth	1.761	1.566	2.178
22.	California State-Sacramento	1.659	1.600	1.786
23.	Portland State	1.590	1.633	1.500
24.	State Univ. College at Buffalo	1.568	1.450	1.821
25.	Georgia State	1.511	1.316	1.929
26.	University of Pittsburgh	1.511	1.150	2.286
27.	Wichita State	1.488	1.500	1.464
28.	University of Colorado-Denver	1.454	1.366	1.643
29.	University of New Haven	1.431	1.199	1.929
30.	Univ. of Nebraska-Omaha	1.363	1.200	1.714
31.	Claremont Graduate School	1.352	1.350	1.357

Rank	School	Total Sample	ASC Sample	ACJS Sample
32.	University of South Florida	1.352	1.316	1.429
33.	Western Illinois	1.204	.8333	2.000
34.	Eastern Illinois University	1.181	.9333	1.714
35.	Pepperdine University	1.181	1.200	1.143
36.	Sangamon State	1.181	.9333	1.714
37.	Nova University	1.159	.9333	1.643
38.	California State-Fresno	1.125	1.016	1.357
39.	Florida International	1.125	1.166	1.036
40.	University of Mississippi	1.068	.6166	2.036
41.	Indiana Univ. of Penn.	.9722	.5000	2.000
42.	Central Missouri State	.9318	.5500	1.750
43.	Jacksonville State	.9203	.7332	1.322
44.	Southern Mississippi	.8296	.4000	1.750
45.	Louisiana State	.8181	.5666	1.357
46.	Northern Arizona	.7840	.6834	1.000
47.	Akron College	.7613	.4999	1.321
48.	Xavier University	.7613	.4166	1.500
49.	Auburn-Montgomery	.7613	.4166	1.500
50.	University of Toledo	.7499	.6000	1.072
51.	Missouri-Kansas City	.7386	.4833	1.286
52.	Long Island Univ.-Brooklyn	.7045	.5500	1.306
53.	Texas A & I University	.7044	.4833	1.179
54.	Oklahoma City	.6591	.5667	.8570
55.	Arkansas-Little Rock	.6136	.4666	.9290
56.	Chapman College	.6022	.6000	.6070
57.	Mercy College	.5681	.4000	.9290
58.	East Texas State	.5113	.5000	.5360
59.	Rollins College	.5113	.6000	.3210
60.	Clark University	.5000	.4499	.6070
61.	Troy State-Troy	.5000	.2167	1.107
62.	West Chester	.4886	.2500	1.000
63.	California Lutheran College	.4885	.3333	.8210
64.	Troy State-Montgomery	.4772	.2333	1.000
65.	Salve Regina-Newport College	.3750	.2500	.6430
66.	West Georgia College	.3750	.3000	.5350
67.	Oregon College	.3636	.2166	.6790
68.	Northeast Louisiana	.3522	.1000	.8920
69.	Long Island Univ.-Greenvale	.3295	.2333	.5360
70.	Webster College	.3181	.2333	.5000
71.	American Technological University	.1136	.1000	.1430

Source: DeZee, Matthew R. "The Productivity of Criminology and Criminal Justice Faculty." June 1980, p. 18-20. Prepared for the Joint Commission on Criminal Justice Education and Standards. U.I.C.

ing the 1960's and 1970's were noted. A study of doctoral graduates from six institutions conducted by George Felkenes (1980) revealed that the majority, 70 percent, were currently employed in the educational field. The six institutions, all of which offered doctorates in criminology or criminal justice, were the University of California at Berkeley, Sam Houston State, State University of New York at Albany, Michigan State University, Florida State University, and the University of Maryland. All of these programs existed prior to the advent of L.E.A.A., and all had made a commitment to education in criminal justice. With the exception of the State University of New York at Albany, all offered undergraduate degrees in criminology or criminal justice.

A study of the prestige of graduate programs in criminology and criminal justice conducted by DeZee (1980) placed all of these programs in the best ten programs in the country. Berkeley was not included, because the School of Criminology was closed in 1975. Of particular interest in the studies of Felkenes and DeZee is the identification of established programs in criminology and criminal justice which are graduating individuals who will serve as both educators and practitioners.

Table II-3 provides the rankings of the 71 institutions by members of A.S.C. and A.C.J.S. included in DeZee's study. Most programs in the upper level of DeZee's prestige rankings had their beginnings prior to the inception of the L.E.E.P. program.

In many ways graduate program development in criminal justice continues to be in transition. Several institutions are planning to implement doctoral programs in criminal justice in the future, and a great many more are reviewing current graduate programs with a view toward modification. Although most of the contemplated changes relate to course content and curricula, a number of other issues are being explored, such as the value of internships and life experience.

Criticism of graduate education in criminal justice may be likened to that of undergraduate education, for many of the issues are the same for both: the quality of the faculty and student body, the use of adjuncts or part-time professors, inadequate institutional support, and poorly designed curricula. Many of the criticisms levelled at graduate education in criminal justice are also of concern in other disciplines. David Riesman (1976) has written that the emphasis on "courting" graduate students and students' hostility to research are threatening the quality of graduate education. Criticism of Nova College's off-campus graduate programs is not limited to criminal justice (Drake, 1979). Sam (1979) has questioned the granting of credit for life experience, in an article entitled, "Life Experience--An Academic Con Game," he suggested that granting such credit was adopted to increase declining enrollments and thereby avoid job losses.

The issues are real and no less important because they affect other disciplines and other aspects of the academic community. However, the problems facing criminal justice higher education are not unique to the field but are shared with other fields in many ways.

THE END OF THE BEGINNING

In a study of criminal justice education, *Criminal Justice Education: The End of the Beginning* (1980), conducted under the auspices of John Jay College of Criminal Justice, the authors concluded that the field has moved into a new phase of development:

> It was found, contrary to prior expectation, that vocationalism in criminal justice education is on the wane and that a strong trend toward academic education is firmly established. These trends may dominate developments in the field during the next five to ten years, and they have important implications for educational quality, for the nature of the faculty in criminal justice programs, for faculty scholarship in a field that places emphasis on teaching, and for the relationships between colleges and criminal justice agencies. Criminal justice education has, in a relatively brief period, reached the end of the beginning. It is well established in American postsecondary education and is well embarked on what will be, inevitably, a long period of development (p. 130).

Research conducted by the Joint Commission tends to support many of the findings of the John Jay study. There is evidence that criminal justice education is beginning to mature and gain acceptance as a relative newcomer to the academy. If so, the field must break its ties with certain aspects of the past and face the future as an equal partner in the educational enterprise. Change cannot be accomplished without an understanding of the past and of the issues that have contributed to concern about the lack of quality within criminal justice education. In order to understand the past, an exploration from several perspectives of the multifaceted aspects of quality in higher education will be necessary.

Chapter III

ISSUES IN CRIMINAL JUSTICE EDUCATION

Standards may be viewed as those individual elements that contribute to the judgment and evaluation of quality. Much has been written about their historical development, and even more has been said about their present meaning and applicability. A standard is generally thought of as an agreed upon principle or as a goal to be attained. In recent years, much of the literature in higher education has addressed an apparent relaxation of standards (Ainsworth, 1977; Day, 1977; Sanoff, 1980). As benchmarks of tradition, standards came under attack from students and faculty in the 1960's and 1970's. A standard implied an elitist view of quality and suggested the attempt to mold individuals to a preconceived and perhaps irrelevant model of behavior. Hartle, Baratz, and Crafa have argued:

> The present interest in identifying, tightening, or clarifying the elements of a college education stems from developments of the 1960's. During this decade colleges and universities were pressed by political protest and the increasing enrollments of non-traditional students to change curricula (Hartle, et al. 1979, p.56).

The new search for standards has institutional, faculty, and government support but to say that all standards are easily measurable or pedagogically sound contributes to a specious argument. When other academic disciplines have explored the need for minimum standards, the primary thrust has been toward measurable variables: direct support services such as counseling and library resources, the number of students per faculty member, and the degrees earned by faculty members. Olscamp justifies a quantitative approach on political grounds:

> In my experience, quantitative analysis is easier to perform than qualitative analysis and is more effective with trustees and legislators. Therefore, quanitative analysis is the path we should follow, provided we do not permit a confusion of accountability with judgments of justification (Olscamp, 1976, p.197).

Few, if any, professional academic associations seek to analyze the philosophical nature of the academic enterprise within the classroom, and a general reluctance to address specific issues of curricula is evident. Except in a very general way, these areas are largely viewed as the province of the faculty.

In attempting to understand the minimum standards debate, education must recognize the environment in which criminal justice programs were established and developed; the nature of the institutional and financial support for these programs; the changing nature of the student body; the desired outcomes of these programs which may have changed over time; and the state of the art today. Recognition of these issues raises the question: Does a need for minimum standards exist? Attempts to answer this question have been made with much difficulty. What Olscamp has called the "language of quality" (1976, p. 197) is often opaque to non-academics and obscure even to full-time educators. Moreover, few have been able to agree on the overall scope that minimum standards should take. Should one seek a program of learning common to all disciplines (the "Renaissance Man" approach), or should one teach specific skills such as reading, writing, and mathematics (the "Literate Man" approach)? (Hartle, et al. 1979, p.57).

The Joint Commission's effort began with the premise that a large number of individuals interested in and involved with criminal justice and criminology in higher education are concerned about the quality of their own programs. This premise is based upon a number of well documented surveys of the field (The Joint Commission sponsored studies by DeZee (1980) on faculty productivity, Felkenes (1980) on doctoral programs, and Culbertson and Carr (1981) on curricula. See also the opinions expressed in C. Allen Pierce's working paper, "Impact of Police Higher Education Programs on Values and Attitudes of Their Students," (especially pp. 61-71). If a consensus occurs among educators that minimum standards are important, further research and analysis might lay the groundwork for the adoption of a set of minimum standards that are acceptable to the vast majority of those concerned.

CONCEPTS, DATA, AND IMPLICATIONS

The approach of the Joint Commission is premised on the following concepts. First, the Commission recognized that criminal justice education is problematic. Conscious efforts at improving the quality of education in criminal justice are in order, and one mechanism for improvement is the establishment of minimum standards for the field. Second, although the need for standards is recognized, the exact nature of appropriate standards for the field is unknown. Third, the systematic research, which carefully describes and analyzes the present state of the art in criminal justice education, should produce information capable of assisting in the formulation of a set of minimum standards appropriate for the field.

A broadly based study design was employed to identify and produce data on as many of the principal issues as possible and to merge the data into a research survey to provide the Commission with information about the state of the field. An effort was made to focus on the myths and the realities of criminal justice higher education. Through various research methodologies, a series of variables upon which standards might be based was identified, and through an iterative process, a series of recommendations for minimum standards was established. The Commission's recommendations aim to assist criminal justice programs in their future development. Surprisingly, the Commission found a wide range of adherence to what might be termed acceptable academic standards. On the other hand, in the minds of Commission members little doubt exists that a number of criminal justice programs in the United States still leave much to be desired, and much remains to be done if the entire field is to reach generally accepted levels of quality.

The standards proposed by the Joint Commission are minimal. They represent a consensus on the part of the Commission and what educational leaders in the field believe a program should "look like." Programs may meet standards in alternative ways, and in today's educational environment, alternative forms of education may require different measures of performance. Nevertheless, the Commission does feel that for most programs the standards outlined in this book are both reasonable and necessary.

Finally, establishing minimum standards cannot be undertaken in a vacuum. The decision to upgrade the quality of criminal justice education unfortunately comes at a time when the prospering years of higher education are at an end, and most universities and colleges are undergoing dramatic changes resulting from financial problems. Because American colleges and universities have always been the subject of scrutiny and debate, the ability to make meaningful changes in criminal justice education, especially as they relate to funding, will be extremely difficult. Although many of the recommendations of the Joint Commission have fiscal implications, many also require a strong professional commitment. No set of standards will have a positive impact unless the field itself is prepared to undertake the difficult task of making the many changes required to implement the standards. Although the Commission did not take a position on implementation, a chapter has been devoted to it.

Prior to the work of the Joint Commission, at least seventy standards for criminal justice education had been developed by others concerned with this issue. The Joint Commission relied heavily on those standards to provide guidance in its own efforts. Many of the Commission's recommendations are reaffirmations of standards developed by other groups as well as the results of the Commission's research and discussions.

THE ISSUE OF QUALITY

At the heart of the work by the Joint Commission was an emphasis on means of improving quality in criminal justice education. In many ways quality is an elusive term, difficult to identify and frequently perceived differently by individuals. Within higher education a large amount of scholarly writing has addressed the issue of quality. "The effort to identify the elements of a good education and find a sure way of providing them has a long history." (Hartle, et al., 1979, p.56). The so-called measures by which quality is determined take many forms including selectivity of institutions (Astin and Solmon, 1979). The problem of measuring quality is complicated, but as Olscamp writes:

> First, quality indeed exists, and it can be talked about and described. But the language of quality is so difficult, and so few people outside the full-time faculties and staffs of colleges have the opportunity and motive to learn it, that it is for all intents and purposes ineffective as a tool for purposes of accountability and budget presentation (Olscamp, 1976, p.197.).

In a later article Olscamp concludes that program quality can not be quantified. Nevertheless, he states that a definition of what contributes to the presence or absence of quality can be made, and "to create a high quality program we would need to know what properties or attributes the program would require in order to cause the properties of quality graduates to come into being" (Olscamp, 1978, pp. 505,508). In some sense Olscamp's approach to understanding quality provides the basis for efforts to improve the quality of higher education.

Hartle, Baratz, and Crafa (1979) found that the states are increasingly interested in identifying, tightening and clarifying the elements of a college education:

> Support for more standards is widespread. Most states noted that the governor, the state department of education, the board of higher education, individual institutions, faculty and students back the movement towards standards. In several states the driving force came from administrators at individual campuses, academic deans, and college presidents (p.58).

Their interest is in standards related to the basic skill levels of undergraduates, and they emphasize that the desire to implement standards does not resolve the problem of identifying those standards that are relevant and how they should be used.

Probably the most commonly used measure of quality is that of perception, followed closely by peer evaluation. Astin and Solmon (1979), reporting on research efforts to develop measures of quality, maintain that: "Peer groups and indices of selectivity provide such measures." They note: "Selectivity is widely used as a measure of quality in research studies and is important in predicting student outcomes" (p.50). In regard to peer evaluations they recognize that ratings of graduate departments "have attracted a good deal of attention, but they have also been criticized for a number of methodological reasons" (p.50). Table III-1 illustrates the highest ranking four-year institutions by estimated selectivity over time. One criticism has been the relative stability of institutions at the

TABLE III-1
HIGHEST-RANKING 4-YEAR INSTITUTIONS
BY ESTIMATED SELECTIVITY

Institution	1961-63	Rank In 1973	1976-77	Change In Rank 1961-77
California Institute of Technology	1	1	1	0
Massachusetts Institute of Technology	3	3	5	-2
Swarthmore	4	10	6	-2
Rice	5	22	14	-9
Harvard*	6	5	3	+3
Stanford.	7	20	17	-10
Reed	8	15	28	-20
Amherst	9	4	12	-3
Pomona	10	23	30	-20
Harvey Mudd	11	9	11	0
Carleton	12	24	24	-12
University of Chicago	13	27	21	-8
Haverford	14	8	9	+5
Webb Institute of Naval Architecture	15	6	8	+7
Yale	16	13	4	+12
Princeton	17	11	13	+4
Columbia and Barnard	18	12	10	+8
Middlebury	19	49	42	-23
Wellesley	20	25	32	-12
John Hopkins	21	29	15	+6
Williams	22	26	19	+3

Bryn Mawr	23	17	7	+16
Brandeis	24	34	44	-20
Oberlin	25	39	32	-7
Dartmouth	**	16	16	
Rensselaer Polytechnic Institute	**	18	25	
Duke	**	19	34	
Brown	**	21	22	
Carnegie Mellon	**	33	18	
Cooper Union	**	32	20	
Wesleyan (Connecticut)	**	30	23	
Mount Holyoke	**	35	24	

*Radcliffe College, ranked second in 1961-63, has since merged with Harvard.

**Rank in 1961-63 was below 25, but actual rank is not available.

NOTE: Deep Springs College, ranked second in both 1973 and 1977, is a two-year college. New College, ranked 14th in 1973, has since merged with University of South Florida.

Source: Astin (1965), Astin & Henson (1977), Barron's (1978), and Cass & Birnbaum (1977).

Source: Astin, Alexander W., and Lewis C. Solmon. "Measuring Academic Quality: An Interim Report." Change, Vol. 11: p. 51, Sept. 1979.

top of this list over a long period of time. Astin and Solmon state:

By using a number of different definitions of quality, we expect to be able to develop many different lists of top-ranked institutions. While many of the same institutions will appear in different lists, we expect that the lists will also vary substantially according to the criteria being used and the population being served. We hope that exemplary institutions will be used as models by institutions striving to survive the hard times ahead (Astin and Solmon, 1979, p.50).

TABLE III-2
TOP 15 COLLEGES AND UNIVERSITIES AS DETERMINED BY THE INDEX OF SALARY DISPERSION AND ALTERNATIVE MEASURES OF INSTITUTIONAL QUALITY

Institution Rank	Salary Dispersion Index 1975	Economics	Roose-Anderson Rated Quality of Graduate Faculty, 1969		Gourman Index 1967	Astin Index of Selectivity 1965
			Philosophy	Physics		
1	Yale	Harvard	Princeton	Berkeley (a)	Princeton	CA Inst. of Tech.
2	Harvard	MIT	Harvard	CA Inst. of Tech.	Harvard	MIT
3	John Hopkins	Chicago	Michigan	Harvard (a)	Yale	Rice
4	Princeton	Yale	Pittsburgh	Princeton	Columbia	Harvard
5	Columbia	Berkeley	Cornell	MIT (b)	Chicago	Stanford (b)
6	Chicago	Princeton	Berkeley	Stanford (b)	Notre Dame	Amherst (b)
7	Stanford	Michigan	Yale	Columbia (c)	Stanford	Yale (c)
8	SUNY at Stony Brook	Minnesota	UCLA (d)	Illinois (c)	Dartmouth	Chicago (c)
9	Rutgers	Pennsylvania	Chicago (d)	Chicago (e)	Pennsylvania	Princeton
10	Northwestern	Stanford	Columbia (d)	Cornell (e)	CA Inst. of Tech.	Columbia (f)
11	Brandeis (g)	Wisconsin	Brown (g)	CA, San Diego (g)	UCLA	Duke (f)
12	Dartmouth (g)	Columbia	MIT (g)	Yale (g)	MIT	Dartmouth (h)
13	MIT	Northwestern	Stanford (g)	Wisconsin	Brown	RPI (h)
14	Pennsylvania	UCLA	Texas (j)	Michigan (j)	Rice	Cornell (h)
15	SUNY at Buffalo	Carnegie-Mellon	Wisconsin	Pennsylvania (j)	Univ. of Wash.	Georgetown

(a) Tied for 1st place.
(b) Tied for 5th place.
(c) Tied for 7th place.
(d) Tied for 8th place.

(e) Tied for 9th place.
(f) Tied for 10th place.
(g) Tied for 11th place.
(h) Tied for 12th place.

(j) Tied for 14th place.

Source: Adams, Arvil V., and Joseph Krislov. "Evaluating the Quality of American Universities: A New Approach." Research in Higher Education, Vol. 8 p. 100, 1978.

A similar approach is taken in evaluating the quality of departments within institutions, utilizing peer evaluation and selectivity as measures.

Adams and Krislov (1978) suggest using faculty salaries as a measure of institutional quality. They write:

> The theory of internal wage structures treats the academic institution as an internal labor market with ports of entry, lines of progression, and an administered salary structure. It is the market behavior of academic institutions in this environment seeking to maintain or achieve specific levels of faculty quality which produces the alternative measure of institutional quality (p.98).

Table III-2 lists the top fifteen colleges and universities as determined by Adams and Krislov and that of other researchers including Astin. Of particular interest should be a comparison of the different approaches to measuring quality, both by institution and by department.

Research conducted by Beyer and Snipper (1974) was designed to test objective and subjective indicators of quality in graduate programs. Their measures included participation in professional organizations, percentage of faculty with doctorates, average number of academic jobs held, doctoral education quality, and the pattern of quality of university employees.

Braskamp, Wise, and Hengstler (1979), in a study of undergraduates' and graduates' satisfaction with their majors as a measure of quality, found a high correlation between satisfaction with major and satisfaction with mentorship. No differences were found concerning class level, grade point average, sex, or field of study as influencing factors in students' perceptions of quality. However, Marg (1979) found that the evaluation of teachers by students could be manipulated by reducing the quality of teaching and improving the morale of students.

Other measures of quality based upon objective, measurable factors, such as the number of volumes in a library, counseling support provided to students, student-faculty ratio, class size, grade levels, student entrance scores, and faculty characteristics are commonly used by accreditation groups and by others interested in analyses. Defining quality in any academic pursuit is difficult, and criminal justice is no exception. On the other hand, identifying a lack of quality may be easy:

> To describe quality we are required to describe the types or classes of things with which we are concerned and then to explain what we mean when we say that people or examples among the classes or types are good, better, or best, among them. These descriptions make the matter of quality in higher education mind-boggling; for of all institutions in organized life, institutions of higher education are probably concerned with a wider range of types than any other (Olscamp, 1976 p. 197).

Olscamp's remarks foreshadow the kind of problems faced in any attempt to evaluate present quality and to formulate standards for the future. Throughout the Joint Commission's study, researchers and writers recognized the difficulty of conceptualizing and explaining the issues of quality and standards. The question raised by all studies is: How can subjective impressions be measured objectively? Olscamp recognized the difficulty of qualitative analysis. The Joint Commission's study, however, attempted both methods; that is, to make statements of value from normative observations. By coming to terms with what *is*, the Commission hoped to determine what ought to be.

Chapter IV

IMPLEMENTING MINIMUM STANDARDS

Criminal justice is, in many ways, a unique field within academe and the professions. Although those in the field may learn much from the history of other fields, the problems of implementing minimum standards in criminal justice education will ultimately be determined by the criminal justice faculty and academic administrators.

Minimum standards are designed to correct present deficiencies and to prescribe future performance. To formulate such standards, the realities of a given field of study must be observed and then ways must be developed of moving from those real conditions towards ideal ones. Minimum standards may be considered "valid" then if 1. they take into account empirically verifiable conditions, 2. they propose ideals which can be realistically met, and 3. the progress towards those ideals can be measured and charted. Because the concept of valid minimum standards--with their attendant ideals, goals, and value judgments--is inextricably linked to personal notions of quality, attaining a consensus about what minimum standards should do and how they should be affected is difficult.

TRADITIONAL STANDARDS

Traditionally, educators have sought numerical standards with which to measure abstract ideas of quality. For school or

program accreditation, many educators have considered test
scores, Ph.D. ratios, faculty publications, and other supposed-
ly objective criteria as valid measures of quality. As a result,
accreditation boards and review panels could define specific
areas in need of development; for example, a program in which
students had high test scores but in which faculty publication
records were poor might stimulate a board to develop
minimum standards for faculty performance. Larsen (1974)
has voiced a growing disenchantment with apparently objective ways of assessing subjective value:

> Accreditation decisions for all agencies are too often
> based on elements of institutional form--Ph.D.
> ratios, book counts, curricular requirements, admis-
> sion test scores, and others. These criteria are in-
> creasingly being challenged as unimportant or
> meaningless--little related to the fundamental
> values which the college is trying to achieve; yet,
> they commonly are the only basis available for judg-
> ment (Larsen, 1974, p. 3).

A basic disagreement over general educational purpose also
challenges the validity of traditional minimum standards. Harris (1978) has argued that any standards may be potentially in-
applicable, because the purposes of higher education change
and because the kinds of post-secondary degree programs
grow and diversify. Harris reflects "a general public impression that a qualification from an accredited institution does
not guarantee an acceptable level of competence in a
graduate" (Harris, cited in Simpson, 1979, p. 15). He also
recognizes the "limitations of standardized accreditation procedures" in non-traditional programs of education. The criteria
used to evaluate a traditional campus may not apply to an experimental program. "The structures and processes traditionally used to evaluate higher education," Harris suggests,
"do not have universal application" (ibid., p. 16). In addition,
the interest in competency-based education--which focuses on
skill learning rather than on the formal processes of education--
has also challenged notions of standards. As David Ainsworth
has argued, the problem of maintaining standards in competency based programs is difficult:

> One of the dangers of a competency-based educa-
> tional system is that the unit of certification is sub-
> ject to strong debasing influences. This can result in

a system with excessively low standards, unless the nature of these influences is properly understood and controlled. There are two main debasing influences, one related to the nature of competencies, and one related to the nature of human beings (Ainsworth, p. 327).

Minimum standards are consequently somehow intimately linked to the institutional nature of a program. Expectations, and therefore, ideas of standards differ between one kind of institution and another, for example, a liberal arts college and an urban commuter university. In addition, individual educational philosophies may affect views of minimum standards. Should a program designed to produce technicians be evaluated in the same way as a program designed to produce scholars? For example, how can an undergraduate science program designed to prepare students for medical school be compared with a program designed to prepare its graduates for advanced research work in biology? Because of the differences in educational programs, educational theorists devised three general "models" of educational development each having their own curricular, instructional, and social goals. Pearson (1978) has labeled the models "technical/vocational," "professional/managerial," and "humanistic/social." The first two models are forms of what Tenney (1971) considered "applied education" (Simpson, 1979).

> Training curricula emphasize the immediate job environment in the practitioner or would-be practitioner...Professional curricula also display a job-related concern. The difference is that these focus upon theoretical and practical aspects of human behavior and interpersonal relationships (Simpson, p. 70, discussing Tenney, 1971).

The "humanistic/social" model, however, attempts to orient students towards theory and towards a more holistic view of their disciplines than either of the applied models. The third model does not "attempt to develop skills or knowledge directly related to performance of any job function" (Simpson, 1979, p. 70). Rather, it attempts to foster a greater understanding of the discipline and its value to society.

Simpson and others have discussed the relative merits of

these three models and their implications for criminal justice minimum standards implementation. These models are discussed in Chapter VI. Any minimum standards developed for the field must take account of the educational models proposed for the field. The problem is not that minimum standards *cannot* be developed for the field; rather, it is that minimum standards can be developed only when a general consensus is reached about the field's educational purpose, models or goals. Ending the debate between criminology and criminal justice may not be necessary, or deciding whether crime-related programs should be vocational, professional, or narrowly academic is not required. If people in the field can agree on a basic body of knowledge, a body of literature, and methods, then perhaps assessments can begin.

Educational programs have been assessed in various ways and minimum standards have been formulated. They are examined and contrasted to other professional programs, and they suggest opportunities for criminal justice evaluations. Although accreditation has been mentioned, it is but one of four ways of implementing minimum standards. These include:

1. Specialized accreditation
2. Voluntary peer review
3. Standards for program development
4. Professionalization.

Each form of implementation defines a program's relationship to the university, to the professional organizations, and to the government. One kind of implementation may be selected not because it does justice to the field but because it gives teachers an autonomy from federal, state, agency, and institutional control. This problem is explored in detail in Chapter V.

SPECIALIZED ACCREDITATION

In his monograph for the Joint Commission, Antony Simpson traced the development of systems of accreditation for higher education and contrasted the problems of accrediting criminal justice programs with that historical development. (Simpson, 1979). Simpson emphasized the relationships of professionals to institutions and of professional organizations to government agencies. His opening chapters delineate the conflicts between agencies and the public interest. Simpson demonstrates how governmental systems of accreditation were invariably linked with governmental financing, either through G.I. Bill grants to students or federal funding to institutions and programs (see especially pp. 11-13). After the Korean War, the government issued a mandate that "federal funds be made available only to institutions of higher education acccredited by organizations deemed to be nationally recognized for this purpose" (p. 12). A cycle was created; to compete for federal financial support, institutions had to gain accreditation from organizations which themselves had to seek federal approval of their function. Simpson's quotation from Zook may be a controlling thesis for any review of accreditation as a means of developing minimum standards:

> Fear of government intervention in educational affairs and yet a realization that there must be some means of educational control and guidance produced the accrediting agency (Zook, 1934, p. 17; quoted in Simpson, 1979, p. 8).

Acknowledging that conflicting organizations compete for professional and financial autonomy, Simpson analyzes two examples of professionalization and specialized accreditation: law and public administration. His purpose is to contrast "an established profession (law) that long ago achieved a mechanism of specialized accreditation largely controlled by an organization of practitioners" with a newly established profession (public administration) in which "accreditation standards [are] administered and controlled by professional schools" (Simpson, 1979, p. 7). For the field of law, the American Bar Association (A.B.A.) and American Association of Law Schools (A.A.L.S.) attempt to control the standards of the professional schools as well as monitor the ethical and professional behavior of member-lawyers. Such a system of control, Simpson suggests, creates an innately conservative field. Law school curricula remain unchanged; legal practitioners are slow to adapt to new social pressures; the professional organizations remain defenders of moral values in a society that makes new demands on the profession by challenging those values (pp. 24-30).

The field of public administration, however, is struggling for identity. Unlike the field of law, no crystallized body of knowledge, belief, or curricular and professional paradigms exist for it. The self-assessed professional status of public administration educators is acknowledged to be low. Because of the diversity among practitioners and educators (or perhaps, in concurrence with this diversity), schools of public administration vary greatly in their curricula and foci. As a result, the establishment of minimum standards and the nationwide accreditation of schools become a problem--how can standards be established for a field in which little consensus exists about the very definition of that field and its practitioners. Simpson notes the growing opposition to any form of accreditation of public administration programs: "The existence of substantial diversity among education programs in the field serves to create opposition to accreditation, based on fears that such a step would lead to the imposition of standards of 'stultifying conformity'" (p. 38; paraphrasing Schott, 1976, p. 255). Opposition to accreditation among public administrators is substantial, Simpson reports (p. 38, citing Engelbert, 1977a).

Simpson's views about criminal justice accreditation grew directly from his perceptions of the different problems faced by public administration and law. He concentrates, however, on the unique relationship between criminal justice and federal organizations like L.E.A.A. He restates earlier complaints that the availability of federal dollars created criminal justice programs with unfounded principles and spare resources; he cites Misner's remarks about "an awful lot of hustlers, and some college presidents serving as pimps,...all looking for the L.E.E.P. dollar" (p.78). Moreover, Simpson voices concern over the relationship between individual programs and those professional organizations that wish to regulate those programs. Simpson's study reveals that the interdisciplinary state of the field has created a wide diversity of opinion on everything from the educational model to curriculum development to the concept of professionalization. However, accreditation in criminal justice programs must contend with the accreditation procedures of universities and colleges where those programs exist. Accreditation processes can and do give the impression of the field's professionalization, its independence, its concern with quality, and its objective review of programs and practitioners. Nevertheless, formal accreditation can make a program dependent on the opinions of outside reviewers, themselves biased either by agency affiliation (if the program is wholly academic) or by traditional academic viewpoints (if the program is vocational in design). Formal accreditation also costs money. If the university pays for it, financial pressures may engender conflict between the program and the institution. If the state or federal government pays for it, the autonomy of the program is lessened, and the program is made responsible to outside sources of funding for its accreditation.

Although accreditation remains the most obvious and widespread way of implementing minimum standards, other innovative techniques exist. These implementations, including outside professional review and inside peer evaluation, may avoid one major problem of accrediting a new and growing field. As Simpson concludes:

> It has yet to be proven that the guidelines that have been developed (for criminal justice) will be successful in their objectives. The danger is that in their application they may become so general as to be little better than those mandated in the generalized accrediting processes colleges have accepted for many years (pp. 81-82).

Moreover, these alternative implementations may allow the field some independence from one group or association as the sole accrediting organization. Simpson feels that the system of peer review practiced by some schools of public administration could have a limited applicability to criminal justice programs and that peer review would remove some of the stigma that formal boards of accreditation bring to the field of criminal justice. Sagarin is vehement in his opposition to formal accreditation. "Criminology is not medicine," he writes, indicating that no one needs a license to practice criminology. "An interest, ability, and facilities should be enough" (Sagarin, 1980, p. 294). Accreditation implies a technical service to Sagarin: "I see a much greater social need for the accreditation of schools of automobile mechanics and television repair persons than of schools or programs for criminologists" (ibid.). In trying to establish accreditation, Sagarin sees active bids for power by forces "less equipped and less capable than ourselves" whose sole purpose is to seek aggressively "to become official accreditors of criminology programs" (ibid.).

PEER REVIEW

Formal peer review is a unique way of evaluating the quality of a program in public administration. It is similar to accreditation, for it involves a national association establishing minimum standards for the field as a whole, which individual

schools must meet. By its very title, peer review suggests a
method of preserving professional autonomy from outside
governments and agencies, but not much literature exists on
the subject.

Peer review was developed by the National Association of
Schools of Public Affairs and Administration (N.A.S.P.A.A.).
It was designed only for programs at least four years old,
although new programs can be granted "provisional" status.
The Association's role in the design and management of individual programs, however, is deliberately limited; its standards report reads:

> The primary concern of these standards is to
> achieve high quality professional education for per-
> sons entering public service. Flexibility and innova-
> tion in curriculum design and means of delivery are
> necessary in order to meet the diverse educational
> needs of full-time and part-time students, pre-entry
> and in-career students, changing career students,
> and students with interests in different career
> specialities...(National Association of Schools of
> Public Affairs and Administration, Standards for
> Professional Master's Degree Programs in Public
> Affairs and Administration, p. 1)

"Flexibility and innovation" are the key terms in the Association's view of curricula. It views the individual program as
always subject to the changing needs of students and the
changing nature of the profession. Unlike the field of law,
which views its curriculum as a canon and its profession as
static, public administration admits to a certain respon-
siveness to social change and public interest. The peer review
process by its very nature embodies a *commitment to adapta-
tion.*

The Association's minimum standards for faculty do not
reflect any absolute standards of faculty achievement but
rather reflect a conception of students' needs. The Association
maintains that half of all courses must be taught by full-time
faculty, not due to any absolute sense of instructional quality
but rather because of its view of the *importance to the student*
of exposure to full-time faculty. As long as a faculty member is
full time, that individual may lack a degree: "Any full-time
faculty member lacking the terminal degree must have a
record of outstanding professional or academic experience

directly relevant to the faculty member's assigned responsibilities" (ibid., p. 3).

Similarly, the Association's view of students is flexible and accommodating. Its report states that admission shall normally (authors' emphasis) be limited to those with an accredited B.A., but also recognizes the possibility of accepting students with different kinds of backgrounds. Although the Association does list five specific criteria for student admission (grades, rank, test scores, biographical information, recommendations), it emphasizes flexibility, with a commitment to overall quality rather than statistical conformity: "Final judgment on admission should be based on a combination of several of the above indicators rather than on a single criterion, with the purpose of increasing the quality of professional personnel entering the public service" (ibid., p.4). Clearly, the N.A.S.P.A.A.'s primary commitments are to accommodate resources to students, to develop innovative curricula, to reflect a changing field and society, and to award degrees to future managers and leaders of quality.

The rhetoric of the N.A.S.P.A.A. is very different from that of the A.B.A., and Simpson also noticed sharp differences in the tone of the two professional organizations. One strives for conformity, the other seeks innovation; one finds quality in established tradition, the other seeks quality in the promise of student and faculty creativity.

STANDARDS FOR PROGRAM DEVELOPMENT

Standards for program development attempts to promulgate minimum standards in the form of policy recommendations. The recommendations of the National Advisory Committee on Higher Education for Police Officers formulated by Lawrence Sherman (1976) and some of the recommendations of the National Manpower Survey of the Criminal Justice System (1976) constituted policy recommendations. Minimum standards represent targets toward which program development activities may aim. The goal is not merely the improvement of individual programs but the improvement of the criminal justice field as a whole. No formal evaluation or compliance is involved, and implementation depends upon the logical appeal of standards to those in institutional authority. Sherman's rationale for developing recommendations is founded on a philosophical approach to quality in education and a strong awareness of the need for authorities to enact recommendations:

> The commission's recommendations rest on the premise that more and better higher education may be the key to producing the personal qualities necessary for police officers to create a new role for the police institution. ...We direct our recommendations for changing police education to the major institutional actors who now control it (Sherman 1978, p.2).

Sherman's educational philosophy is based upon traditional notions of quality, while acknowledging the historical development of specific ways of achieving quality:

> The quality of higher education can be measured only in reference to a set of objectives. Since the time of Aristotle, however, opinions have differed on the objectives of higher education (p. 39).

Sherman's idea of establishing objectives posits a system of goals towards which any educational activity, regardless of discipline, may aspire. However, standards for program development ultimately reflect an implicit philosophy of education and a view of educational improvement as a continuing process. If quality can only be measured by referring to objective standards, as Sherman maintains, then the formulation of those objective standards should take into account the abilities and the limitations of administrators charged with their implementations and of students towards whom they are directed.

Standards for program development are postulated on a notion of self-improvement; given direction, an individual or institution will naturally desire to improve. The standards imply a fundamentally optimistic view of human--and institutional--nature, because "progress" is somehow inherently better than stasis.

Critics argue that the realities of standards of development are less than encouraging. Meeting standards is strictly voluntary, with little external pressure involved, and programs that are far from meeting a given set of standards will probably not engage actively in improving themselves. Hefferlin has made a succinct statement about the relationship between academic reform and external pressure; to him, program change is seldom initiated from within an institution, and the processes of development are rarely successful without some kind of outside intervention: "...the source of academic change has always been and continues to be predominantly outside the educational system..." (Hefferlin, 1969, pp. 39-40). Traditional pleas for faculty autonomy and for professional independence must be made with an awareness of self-deception. Without external evaluation, independent, autonomous misperception, misdefinition, and misinterpretation of standards can flourish. Who reviews the reviewers when faculty comes to believe that they have met or exceeded standards when in fact they have not? Standards that exist solely in the form of recommendations may be adopted only by those programs that already meet those standards. Their adoption may reinforce existing success without promoting future development.

PROFESSIONALIZATION

Working from the theories of Hall (1977), Reed Adams attempted to identify levels of professional commitment among criminal justice personnel. He argued that criminology and criminal justice are professions, because their practitioners display the behavioral traits of other professionals (Adams, 1976). For Frank Morn, the history of a profession is written in the history of its professional organizations (Morn, 1980). To him, the history of medicine could be written by preparing a history of the A.M.A. Morn finds much evidence for the professionalization of criminology and criminal justice in the proliferation of organizations representing the field. Historically, criminology and criminal justice could be considered professions solely because an American Society of Criminology (A.S.C.) and an Academy of Criminal Justice Sciences (A.C.J.S.) exist. Most writers associate professionalization with the founding of what Morn calls "certified professional schools" (Morn, 1980, p. 22). For Hall, however, professionalism is less a matter of institutionalization and more a matter of social behavior. Criteria such as full-time work, training models, associates, and codes of ethics become ways of determining the existence of a profession and the commitment of its members.

Regoli and Miracle, in a Joint Commission report, attempted to measure empirically the levels of professionalization in the field. By collecting data on individual educators' commitments to professional organizations, belief in public service, sense of calling, journal publications, and other variables, they established quantifiable degrees of professionalism. Unlike Morn, Adams, and others, Regoli and Miracle "avoid discussing whether or not a particular occupation (e.g., criminal

justice educators) is a profession but rather identify where an
occupation lies on the continuum" (p. 12).

All these studies of professionalism postulate a set of norms
or standards against which an individual's professional commitment may be measured and through which the professionalization of an entire field may be assessed. These viewpoints have within them a concept of minimum standards and
a set of value judgments about the quality of a discipline and
the achievements of its members. DeZee's study, for example,
concentrates on a single aspect of faculty behavior ("productivity" measured by journal publication) to assess the quality
of a program and the professional status of its faculty. DeZee
agrees with Oronamer that "the nature and quality of
academic departments will in large measure determine the
future development of the discipline" (DeZee, 1980, p. 8, citing
Oronamer, 1970, p. 243). In many ways, the achievements and
activities of a criminal justice faculty do determine outside
perceptions of the field's quality. The serious criticisms levelled at the quality of the faculty (e.g., too many agency personnel, too few doctorates, not enough research) often reflect on
the status of the field as a whole. The caliber of department
and discipline prestige (a subjective measurement) frequently
depends on perceived levels of faculty ability and productivity
(objective measurements) (see DeZee, p. 10). The difficulty of
formulating objective standards from subjective self-
assessments further complicates any professional approach to
minimum standards implementation.

POLITICS OF MINIMUM STANDARDS

The development and implementation of minimum standards for criminal justice education impinge on some political
processes. The control of minimum standards necessarily involves outside professional organizations whose interests or
commitments to quality may be affected by their overall concern with what Sagarin has seen as power plays. The relationship between the two major organizations in criminal justice
(A.S.C. and A.C.J.S.) has created tensions not only within the
field's organization but, as Regoli and Miracle have noted, in
the very minds of the profession's members. The existence of
these two organizations complicates the field's sense of identity. Morn holds the view that two professional organizations
imply two professions. Sagarin argues that, regardless of the
existence of A.S.C. and A.C.J.S., "no consensus exists as to

what constitutes criminology or who is a criminologist" (1980, p. 296). Sagarin's forecast is glum:

> ...Criminologists and administrators have a great deal to learn from each other, a great deal to offer in the way of mutual assistance. And, while within a single organization they may argue, in two organizations they might not speak at all. They certainly would not have the same resources (1980, p. 300).

Any effort to implement minimum standards will be less than successful if these two organizations fail to agree about standards and their implementation procedures. The need for consensus is immediate, because these two organizations have an almost equivalent size and membership composition. If standards are to have any impact at all on the field, the members of both organizations will have to accept individual standards and their mode of implementation.

Not only must standards be acceptable to the field, they must be acceptable to the students and faculty whose programs they affect directly. Standards that are developed without involving students and faculty would violate basic principles of autonomy and self-determination. Most likely, a compromise will be effected between acceptability and utility. If standards are set too high, they are likely to be rejected by most programs that fail to meet them. If standards are too low, not only would they be ineffective in improving the field's quality, but they would likely be unacceptable to effective programs and leading educators. Standards that are barely acceptable but weak will only contribute to perpetuating a myth that the field is undergoing significant, comprehensive analysis. Not only will weak standards be meaningless, they will be self-defeating. A major political issue in the implementation of minimum standards, therefore, lies in the differences in acceptability between programs that now meet or exceed standards and programs that would fail to meet them. The politics of minimum standards also involves acceptability of procedures by other groups and organizations. A growing number of college and university administrators resist specialized accreditation due to the costs involved and due to concern for federal funding dependent upon accreditation. The field of criminal justice must develop its own standards and monitor its own programs. Although the sacrifice of professional autonomy for financial reward may immediately tempt some, programs may have to pay a larger debt by failing to develop their own acceptable approach, whether it be accreditation or some other form of implementation.

Chapter V

INSTITUTIONAL SUPPORT FOR CRIMINAL JUSTICE EDUCATION

A review of the development of criminal justice programs supports the belief that general college and university administrators were instrumental in introducing courses and programs on their campuses. Although the reasons for supporting these programs may have been prompted by an interest in securing federal funds, support for the concept of a new field of study was the end result.

Criticism of administrative choices to establish criminal justice programs has frequently been aimed at the budgetary nature rather than at the academic or educational value of the decisions. In fact, some would believe that such decisions were somehow unique to criminal justice programs. They were not, because virtually all new academic programs introduced on American campuses in 1960's and 1970's have been related to decisions about the allocation of scarce resources.

What may have been unique about criminal justice programs was the relatively large amount of federal funding made available for their development in a short period of time. The rapid growth of the field contributed to problems and confusion that did not accompany other areas of study which grew more slowly. Furthermore the role of the academic administrator has changed and should not be overlooked in attempting to understand the rapid development of criminal justice programs. From beginnings in the 17th century, the role of the university administrator has evolved through various stages which may be viewed as spiritual leadership (Edwards at Princeton), autocratic reform (Elliott at Harvard, Harper at Chicago), technocratic management (Seaborg at California), and recently as what might be termed bureaucratic entrenchment against student and faculty initiative (see, for example, Clark Kerr's 1972 lecture on *Conflict, Retrenchment, and Reappraisal,* 1979, hereafter cited as Kerr, 1972). Kerr saw the administrator as a manager of conflict as early as 1972. As universities grew in size and scope and as the jobs of presidents and deans began to include fund raising, financial management, and organizational skills, the image of the administrator became similar to the image of the corporate president.

The function of the contemporary administrator extends beyond the boundaries of the university, and as his administrative power is delegated to vice presidents, provosts, deans, and others, the administrator has come to assume new and broader ranged activities. Today's administrator must look outward towards the community, the economy, and the federal government as well as inward towards students, faculty and the development of programs at the institution. Criminal justice programs began to appear in universities at a time of great administrative conflict and change.

Sherman (1978) maintains that university administrators were probably responsible for the development of more criminal justice programs than either faculty or students. The primary reason for administrative involvement was funding. L.E.E.P. provided new sources of federal money for students and programs at a time when many institutions faced financial as well as academic crises. Administrators welcomed the opportunity to increase enrollments at little cost. Sherman argues, "In every case, it seems reasonable to assume that the academic administrator has been the central source of support within a college for creating a police-oriented program" (Sherman, 1978, pp. 15-16).

Faculty response to administrators' initiatives varied from apathy to antagonism, but generally the response was one of benign neglect. Many criminal justice programs were established outside of the regular academic structure, frequently through the appointment of a program director or coordinator who did not enjoy the prestige or authority of a traditional department chairman. Many of the directors of criminal justice programs reported directly to an administrator outside the usual chain of command. These programs were not established with the traditional academic approach, which would have required months if not years. Criminal justice programs were established very quickly, but because they required major curricular additions and other organizational arrangements, little time was available to follow the usual academic route for implementation.

> During normal times...the major process of academic change is that of accretion and attrition; the slow addition and subtraction of functions to existing structures. Accretion and attrition are the most common means of academic change primarily because they are the most simple. Unlike radical reform, they are small-scale, undramatic, and often unpublicized. By accretion an institution merely encompasses a new program with the old--a new occupational course, a research project, a new undergraduate tradition (Hefferlin, 1969, pp. 24,25.).

Another problem was the injection of "different" students into the academic mainstream. Usually older and frequently less academically prepared, these students represented new challenges for instructors and in many cases, a new teaching experience. Sherman postulates an alliance between administrators and the criminal justice faculty they hired against the "traditional" academic faculty who were seeing their budgets cut, resources redirected, and power usurped. In many cases, however, the decision by administrators to implement and expand the criminal justice programs was, in fact, designed to assist other disciplines, particularly those that provided service courses within the academic community.

Criminal justice programs frequently reflected the kind of institution in which they were established. In public and community colleges, where most programs were developed, administrators traditionally played a greater role in faculty hiring, firing, and curriculum planning. Jencks and Riesman (1968) maintain that at the private, selective institutions like liberal arts colleges or "multiversities" stronger guidelines were developed for faculty autonomy and professional experience as criteria for departmental decision-making (see also Sherman, 1978, p.199). So-called an "academic revolution," these guidelines gave the faculty political power within the university which promoted the myth of professional privacy. A belief existed that the classroom was closed to administrative interference or outside institutional regulation. The faculty was viewed as having responsibility for all education and for their own professional conscience concerning what they taught. The concept of "academic freedom" frequently became an argument to maintain independence from the administration or federal agencies that wished to regulate or evaluate faculty activities (see Weisman and Holgate, 1979).

Frequently this academic autonomy was not applied to administrators of criminal justice programs. Many of those administrators did not possess traditional academic qualifications: the doctorate and a strong educational background represented by publications and research. Many of them had retired from criminal justice agencies which had permitted less freedom of choice than academe.

In addition to the problems of developing a criminal justice program in what was frequently a hostile environment, newly appointed program administrators often found opposition and criticism from criminal justice agencies within the community that might have been expected to take an interest in the development of a program. The administrators were also accountable to federal agencies from which much of their funding came. The general faculty, however, viewed external influences as a threat to their traditional priorities in curriculum development, hiring, and tenure decisions. All the traditional conflicts between college and community, between professional and scholar, and between teacher and administrator came to the fore as more and more criminal justice programs were developed.

The observations of Baldridge and others (1978) are very relevant to the criminal justice education and administration. Baldridge identifies two opposing poles of administration: autonomy and bureaucracy. An autonomous faculty will make decisions based only on its collective professional expertise and reasoned judgment. When external controls such as deans, agencies, and governmental influences increase, the faculty's autonomy diminishes, and they become bureaucraticized:

> When professional organizations are well "insulated" from environmental influences, then professional values, professional norms, and professional work definitions dominate the processes of

the organization. When external influences increase, the professionals within are frequently reduced to the role of hired employees doing the building of bureaucratic managers, and the level of bureaucratic regulations increases sharply (Baldridge, et. al, 1978, p.119).

The lower the faculty's expertise, the less their power is vis-a-vis administrators and agencies. In a criminal justice department, many members may not possess a doctorate or research experience, and the level of faculty autonomy may be low. That faculty may have to defer to others with more expertise, simply because "expertise buys power in an organization" (Baldridge, et al., 1978, p. 121).

That criminal justice programs actually developed within academe is surprising, yet they actually grew to become an integral part of what was originally a hostile environment. Research conducted by the Commission, tracing this development during the 1960's and 1970's, found a number of changes in recent years that further support the view that criminal justice programs are generally well entrenched, are becoming more traditional in their academic expectations, and are viewed positively by faculty members.

THE ROLE OF THE ACADEMIC ADMINISTRATOR

The administrator of a criminal justice program or unit is charged with three functions. First, the administrator has the responsibility to direct the affairs of the unit by the judicious exercise of authority and persuasion to accomplish the unit's purposes and to obtain its support by society. Secondly, because competing forces may exist among several departments or sections of an institution, the administrator must in general loyalty to the institution make decisions of priority, employing encouragement to weld together in a creative manner the tensions within the unit and between the unit and other parts of the institution that inevitably arise. The third obligation of the administrator has a dual aspect: on the one hand, the administrator is charged with operating with maximum efficiency with available resources; on the other hand, the administrator must obtain adequate resources to fulfill, without sacrifice of integrity or surrender of principle, the unit's total role in society.

The problems of the criminal justice administrator arise

because the job is an exercise in the reconciliation of opposites. In an ideal world of unlimited human material resources, the opposites might coexist without friction. In a practical world, hard choices have to be made. Once those choices have been made, the administrator must make sure by appropriate oversight and control that the unit's purposes are served by the way the resources are used. In addition to facing financial pressures and the need for higher enrollments, the criminal justice administrator must provide the kinds of educational services that local criminal justice agencies want. In many situations criminal justice administrators have been reluctant to make what amounts to strictly academic decisions that would be contrary to the desires of criminal justice agencies. Those decisions involve the development of schedules, the training needs of the local agency, the hiring of faculty, and the granting college credit to agency personnel for little more than attendance at roll call training. The Joint Commission Report recommendations are focused upon facilitating and encouraging criminal justice administrators to actively become leaders in upgrading the quality of criminal justice education programs. Program leaders are encouraged to remain firm and rigourous against pressures by college deans, institution administrators, and agency personnel who may consciously or unconsciously wish to weaken the quality of criminal justice education.

As an academic leader, the criminal justice administrator must articulate the needs of criminal justice education and help shape its general future. Too often criminal justice administrators are not oriented to the future, but tend rather to function with a sense of the past. Too often administrators are surprised by innovations, having no ideas of how to respond to changes in the criminal justice system or academic organization. The academic administrator cannot function without flexibility and innovative alternatives in crisis situations.

To some degree the lack of quality in some criminal justice programs in colleges and universities, the disinterest of potential students for criminal justice careers, and the lack of prestige of criminal justice programs among many faculties can be traced to the need for strong criminal justice education administration.

One perplexing problem facing the Joint Commission was the variety of organizational arrangements and environments within which criminal justice programs operate. Some departments reported directly to a general campus administrator, while others existed within traditional types of structures, operating as a department or as part of a department. Some programs were found to have no academic standing in terms of their privileges within the academic community.

If criminal justice programs are to be accepted and are to achieve an acceptable level of quality, they must be treated in a manner consistent with other, similar programs within the institution. At least one full-time faculty member should be responsible for the program and for its direction. In cooperation with the faculty, this individual should be responsible for formulating departmental policy, developing curricula, and setting academic requirements for students.

The department head must also recognize responsibilities to the academic community. As Baldridge and others have stated, the chairperson has always been a kind of "middle person." In terms of employment, the chairperson has become everything from a supervisor to employee spokesperson to shop steward, a role that has grown important with the increase of faculty unions (Baldridge, et al., 1978 pp. 160-161).

Richard Myren (letter to the Joint Commission, November 5, 1981) identifies the educational leadership of the academic adminstrator as occupying a large percentage of time, with developmental and institutional activities also high on the priority list. Among those activities Myren includes:

A. recruitment of faculty members and working with the faculty who view their specialties within a broad intellectual framework and who are interested in research, teaching and service

B. aiding faculty members with appropriate administrative support in research, teaching, and service

C. making sure that the faculty as a whole not only takes from but contributes to the general intellectual life of the college or university

D. making sure that the faculty continues curriculum development to keep the program alive

E. assisting the faculty in recruitment of high quality students

F. making sure that the faculty sets, achieves and maintains high standards of quality in all of its activities.

When the top administrator has played a stewardship role, decision-making should be placed within the administrator's educational group rather than at a higher level.

RESOURCES

The rapid development of criminal justice programs was frequently characterized by a lack of planning and support services generally accepted as necessary to higher education. Three-fourths of the criminal justice programs in existence in 1970 were less than 6 years old, and 82% of those programs had begun to offer courses within a year after initial planning had begun. (Eastman, 1972, pp. 106; quoted in Sherman, 1978, p. 92).

To understand the administrative relationships and factors affecting administrative support for criminal justice programs, the Commission undertook research to determine how administrations should and do affect the form, content, and purpose of the criminal programs they direct. Questionnaires were sent to a thousand colleges where criminal justice programs had been established. Responding to the survey, administrators at 215 institutions indicated that they had four-year programs. The number of responses from two-year colleges was insufficient to provide a comprehensive analysis. Of 215 four-year programs 62 or 29% offered either a baccalaureate degree or both an associate and a baccalaureate degree. Of these, some programs, 153 or 71%, offered the baccalaureate degree as well as graduate studies leading to a master's or a doctorate. Of this group 153 or 71% were public institutions, and 60 or 28% were private institutions. Two responding institutions indicated that they were funded from both private and public sources.

L.E.E.P. funding was available to students, but very little money was available to fund many of these programs through periods of initial difficulty. Many programs were established with little planning but with the hope that initial enrollments would stimulate increased federal support. Few institutions, apparently, made any long range commitments to criminal justice education, and fewer had any conceptual framework that would give programs meaning and purpose within the academic environment. Table V-1 provides information on the number of institutions receiving L.E.E.P. funding until 1979. Of the institutions surveyed, 85% were receiving L.E.E.P. aid.

Many colleges and universities neglected to provide

students and faculty with resources necessary to accomplish their goals. Because many early criminal justice programs offered courses during evenings, programs were often operated with support services.

TABLE V-1
INSTITUTIONS RECEIVING L.E.E.P. FUNDING
BY TYPE OF INSTITUTIONAL CONTROL

	Public n (%)	Private n (%)	Total n (%)
Received L.E.E.P. Funds	132 (63.5)	44 (21.2)	176 (84.6)
Did not receive L.E.E.P. funds	19 (9.1)	13 (6.3)	32 (15.4)
Total	151 (72.6)	57 (27.4)	208 (100.0)

Concerning services offered to students attending classes during the day, the Commission was disturbed to discover that personal and career counseling were offered only in approximately 80% of the programs surveyed. Academic advising and library resources were available in approximately 95% of the programs. Because many of the students in criminal justice programs were viewed as having remedial deficiences, the Commission was also disturbed to find that only 52% of the programs offered remedial tutoring to criminal justice students. Computer facilities were available to only 71% of the students and computer consultants to only 51%. However, these percentages are probably consistent with services offered to the general student body (see Table V-2). Generally evening students received fewer services than daytime students. (see Table V-3)

Many criminal justice educators have criticized the inadequacy of criminal justice library collections. Writing in 1975, Gordon Misner argued that although most accrediting standards "contained explicit requirements for library investment according to the academic level of the program," apparently no one made sure that those requirements were met:

TABLE V-2
SUPPORT SERVICES PROVIDED TO CRIMINAL JUSTICE
STUDENTS IN DAY PROGRAMS

Service	Offered n (%)	Not Offered n (%)	Don't Know/ Missing n (%)	Total n (%)
Personal Counseling	175 (81.4)	25 (11.6)	15 (7.0)	215 (100%)
Career Counseling	176 (81.9)	25 (11.6)	14 (6.5)	215 (100%)
Academic Advising	202 (94.0)	5 (2.3)	8 (3.7)	215 (100%)
Remedial Tutoring	111 (51.6)	65 (30.2)	39 (18.1)	215 (100%)
Library	205 (95.3)	3 (1.4)	7 (3.3)	215 (100%)
Computer Facilities	154 (71.6)	33 (15.3)	13 (6.0)	215 (100%)
Computer Consultants	111 (51.6)	57 (26.5)	47 (21.8)	215 (100%)

TABLE V-3
SUPPORT SERVICES PROVIDED TO CRIMINAL JUSTICE STUDENTS IN EVENING PROGRAMS

	Offered and Comparable to Daytime Services		Not Offered or Not Comparable to Daytime Services		Don't Know/ Missing		Total	
	n	(%)	n	(%)	n	(%)	n	(%)
Personal Counseling	151	(70.2)	34	(15.8)	30	(14.0)	215	(100.0)
Career Counseling	149	(69.3)	34	(15.8)	32	(14.9)	215	(100.0)
Academic Advising	179	(83.3)	23	(10.7)	13	(6.1)	215	(100.0)
Remedial Tutoring	99	(46.0)	47	(21.9)	69	(32.1)	215	(100.0)
Library	189	(87.9)	12	(5.6)	14	(6.5)	215	(100.0)
Computer Facilities	144	(67.0)	24	(11.2)	47	(21.9)	215	(100.0)
Computer Consultants	103	(47.9)	45	(20.9)	67	(31.2)	215	(100.0)

> Too many programs in the criminal justice field are
> in it primarily for the money and have made no
> significant investment in library resources. We
> could suggest requiring a minimum investment in
> the library prior to the initiation of courses (Misner,
> 1975, p.16).

Some disagreement might arise as to the definition of an adequate library collection, but general agreement exists about
the need for adequate library support. Riddle (1975, p. 30)
states, "The number of students now enrolled in police education programs more than justifies adequate library budgets."

The Joint Commission feels strongly that criminal justice
programs should be on a parity basis with other academic programs and should have the necessary autonomy to realize their
objectives. The library resources necessary to support a program must be available, and when the collection is deficient,
funds must be made available to improve the collection.
Criminal justice faculty must actively recommend the selection of library and other learning resource material needed by
both students and faculty.

Although no data were available by which support services
during the last ten years could be evaluated, the Commission
feels that some progress has been made toward improved support services as programs have gained increased acceptance on
campuses.

FORMS OF SUPPORT

Availability of resources will not transform a mediocre
criminal justice program into a good one, but resources do provide the foundation upon which a good program can be built.
Of particular importance to the future of a criminal justice program is long term institutional support. A secure institutional
commitment will enable a program to survive changes in student enrollments and the whims of federal administrators.
Criminal justice programs can no longer depend upon L.E.E.P.
for their survival, and those institutions that have a commitment to criminal justice education must develop funding that
will maintain quality. Criminal justice faculty should actively
participate in budget preparations, and the program's administrator's participation in the budgeting process should be
consistent with that of other department heads. The criminal
justice department's budget should also be identifiable within

the institution's budget.

Generally, funding for an educational program involves external and internal sources. External support includes grants, federal funding, state and other agency support, and endowments. Internally, an institution may raise funds through tuition and some kinds of state support. The relationship between external and internal financial support frequently reveals the character of an administration and an institution. The budgetary crises facing most educational institutions have forced many administrators to make decisions they probably would have considered impossible during the 1960's and 1970's.

Much literature exists on the financial problems of supporting higher education. Bowen, (1978, pp. 141-163) justifies government spending on education by advocating a "return on investment," just as the buying of stock would be justified because of anticipated annual dividends or future resale value. He argues that higher education differs from business because of education's "socially imposed costs." A university's costs are socially imposed because society demands certain services of the institution and its members. Bowen argues that an institution has a responsibility to government as government has a responsibility to higher education. However, colleges and universities have a special need for freedom from governmental control and social pressures:

> Profit-making enterprises are, of course, as concerned as any other organization to protect their freedom of decision and action. However, colleges and universities as centers of teaching and research have special interest in autonomy because of the responsibility to protect freedom of thought from encroachments either of interest groups or government (Bowen, 1978, p. 149).

Universities, while maintaining autonomy, must recognize the importance of their programs to effective and efficient government.

Almost every major study of the criminal justice system during the past twenty years has emphasized the importance of higher education as a means of helping to improve the system. University administrators and faculty governing boards must decide whether or not they choose to expend resources to establish and maintain a criminal justice program. The Commission recognizes that future budgetary constraints faced by administrators will make funding all programs extremely difficult, but difficult decisions must be made about an institution's educational mission. If they are to achieve the highest level of quality possible, criminal justice programs must be funded equally with other programs.

In many reports to the American Council on Education, printed in the publication *Financing Universal Higher Education* (Mushkin, 1972), the authors of those reports viewed the federal government as the ultimate financial arbiter. For non-traditional programs, many administrators asked the government for funding to support faculty, students, and administrators. Mushkin argues that federal and state agencies must supply most of the investment for the future but that universities must develop their own endowments and financial sources. She contrasts the two directions toward which money might flow: 1. toward the operational aspects of higher education like faculty salaries, student aid, physical plant and 2. toward "the processes of reassessment and reconstitution in higher education," thereby implying some new and innovative approaches to financing (Mushkin, 1972, p. 176).

John Porter, arguing that the public community college is probably the most versatile of all post-secondary educational institutions, states that the "two-year community colleges today are the best equipped post-secondary institutions to provide non-traditional approaches to education." (Porter, 1975, p. 210). A large number of criminal justice programs are located in community colleges.

The Commission feels strongly that consideration must be given to increasing the number of full-time faculty members in criminal justice departments. The Commission was encouraged by an apparent increase in the number of full-time faculty during the 1970's. Of the institutions responding to the Commission's survey, 41% indicated they employed between one and four full-time faculty members and 36% employed between five and nine faculty members. Table V-4 provides the distribution of the number of full-time faculty.

With regard to part-time faculty, 80 or 37% of the programs employed between one and four part-time teachers, and 35 programs or 16.3% between five and nine. The Commission feels strongly that every criminal justice program should have at least one full-time faculty member or administrator with primary responsibility for the program (see Table V-5).

TABLE V-4
NUMBER OF FULL-TIME FACULTY
IN CRIMINAL JUSTICE PROGRAMS

	n	%
1 - 4	88	40.9
5 - 9	77	35.8
10 - 14	21	9.8
15 - 19	7	3.3
20 or more	11	5.1
Not reported	11	5.1
Total	215	100.0

$x = 7.2$
$Mdn = 5.2$
$s = 7.6$

TABLE V-5
NUMBER OF PART-TIME FACULTY
IN CRIMINAL JUSTICE PROGRAMS

	n	%
1 - 4	80	37.2
5 - 9	35	16.3
10 - 14	6	2.8
15 - 19	3	1.4
20 or more	11	5.1
None or not reported	80	37.2
Total	215	100.0

$x = 7.1$
Mdn. = 3.9
$s = 10.8$

Both the teaching load of the average faculty member and the faculty/student ratio affect the workload of criminal justice faculty. According to the Commission's administrative survey, approximately 70% of the faculty taught between six and nine course during an academic year, with approximately 18% teaching less than five courses and 15% teaching ten or more. No significant differences were found between teaching loads in public and private institutions (see Table V-6).

The Commission feels strongly that the teaching loads of faculty in criminal justice programs should be no greater than those in other disciplines.

Data on the student/faculty ratio were inconclusive in the administrative survey, but again, the Commission feels that the student/faculty ratio should be consistent with the ratios in other programs and disciplines.

TABLE V-6
ASSIGNED TEACHING LOAD PER ACADEMIC YEAR
BY TYPE OF INSTITUTION
(Semester System)

	Public n (%)	Private n (%)	Total n (%)
Less than 5 courses	25 (17)	11 (19)	36 (17.3)
6 - 9 courses	103 (68)	40 (69)	143 (68.8)
10 or more courses	22 (5)	7 (12)	29 (13.9)
Total	150 (100)	58 (100)	208 (100.0)

Another measure of institutional support is the amount of money provided for faculty development, including anything from funding for attendance at professional conferences to funds for developing research or for participation in faculty training programs. Approximately 17% of the public institutions allowed less than a hundred dollars a year per faculty member for faculty development. Approximately 30% of the institutions surveyed provided three hundred dollars or more for such development. (see Table V-7).

TABLE V-7
AMOUNT OF MONEY ALLOTTED FOR FACULTY
DEVELOPMENT/PER FTE (Full Time Equivalent Student)
BY TYPE OF INSTITUTIONAL CONTROL

	Public n (%)	Private n (%)	Total n (%)
Less than $99	23 (17)	4 (9)	27 (15.1)
$100 - $199	41 (30)	15 (35)	56 (31.3)
$200 - $299	30 (22)	11 (26)	41 (22.9)
$300 or more	42 (31)	13 (30)	55 (30.7)
Total	136 (100)	43 (100)	179 (100.0)

Finally, to offer a quality program successfully, an institution must provide adequate office space, secretarial and clerical support, and a budget for supplies and equipment sufficient to realize the teaching and research mission. These supportive resources should not be less than those allocated for other departments.

OBLIGATIONS

Members of the Commission often debated whether criminal justice education should be professionally oriented, emphasizing technical skills, or should be conceptually oriented, offering a broad, liberal arts education designed to develop the student's logical, analytical, and conceptual abilities. The Joint Commission maintains that criminal justice programs at the undergraduate level should be like any other major and that criminal justice students should be exposed to a variety of course offerings. The Commission agrees with earlier findings (Sherman, 1978) that the number of specialized criminal justice courses should not exceed one quarter of the total course offerings for a degree.

Administrators charged with directing criminal justice programs must set goals consistent with the goals of other disciplines. Bowen has outlined "a catalog of goals" for higher education. His rationale implies a social philosophy that stresses an individual's development and the value of that individual to the whole society:

> The [items in the catalog] constitute the model that many educators adopt when setting educational policy, and then provide the criteria by which educators and others ideally try to judge the performance of higher education ... There is a need for educators to sort out priorities among the goals, to recognize that there are trade-offs among them, and to be realistic about what can and cannot be achieved with the resources that are likely to be available... The goals of higher education are concerned with the development of the full potentialities of human beings and society. The goals correspond closely to the goals of human life (Bowen, 1977, pp. 53-54).

Bowen's goals (pp.55-59) include cognitive learning or the development of verbal, quanitative, and reasoning skills; emotional and moral development or personal self-discovery, human understanding, and value creation and articulation; and practical competence of social integration, citizenship, and the cultivation of ideals of family, community, and personal behavior.

Bowen's work establishes an interaction between the individual and society. Whether criminal justice education is viewed as pre-professional technical training or as a humanistic study of individual crime and social retribution, Bowen's underlying assumptions about the individual's place within a community or society are noteworthy. As Goldstein stresses, policing is but one part, although a central one, of a criminal justice system designed to examine, judge, and attempt to change individual behavior according to social norms (Goldstein, 1977, p. 21). Implicit in Goldstein's view is the importance of reflection and analysis and of understanding the individual as part of a system in change:

> A program of selective studies within the liberal arts...has the greatest potential for equipping police to undertake the constructive analysis of their function and to change in a changing society (p. 296).

Gordon Misner in his book, *Criminal Justice Studies: Their Trandisciplinary Nature,* states, "No one discipline or field of knowledge can possibly lay claim to the totality of thought on such a complex matter as justice or its administration" (Misner, 1981, p. 355). He adds:

> Undergraduate students in justice studies often question the curricular requirements imposed by their course of study, and they allege that certain subject matters have no relevance to their intellectual interest. Many professors would counter with the argument that the complexity and the global nature of justice studies is the crucial justification for a broad liberal arts education...It may be possible for one to be a competent physician, a chemist, an engineer, or an entomologist without having a broad education in the humanities and the social sciences; however, it is not possible to be a serious student of justice studies without such a background (p. 355).

Lawrence Sherman echoes Misner's concern and directs attention to the administrator's role in assuring a broad educational experience:

> To insure breadth of content, faculty and administrators should counsel students out of their frequent inclination to take all of the courses they can in the police education program. Similarly, students should not be forced to spend too much time in directly related courses (1978, p. 87).

The administrator must work with the faculty to shape the curriculum and advise the individual students on how to make the best use of available courses.

The American Academy for Professional Law Enforcement (A.A.P.L.E.) established "Ethical Standards in Law Enforcement" in 1978 and included material on education and training practices. The Academy recognized the importance of a broadly based approach to education:

> Law enforcement instructors should emphasize the ethical responsibility in policing for both the agency and the individual officer. They should encourage students in their quest for knowledge and in their development of professional skills, giving them every assistance in the free exploration of ideas. The quest for truth is essential to the achievement of justice.
>
> The instructor should properly advise students to ensure that they understand opportunities and requirements in the field, as well as limitations.
>
> The instructor, in discussing law enforcement techniques, should impress upon the student the importance and problems of putting theory into practice, of adherence to all applicable principles governing practices, and of the retention of such principles in accord with organization regulations.
>
> An instructor of law enforcement should stress to the students the importance of the systems contexts in which criminal justice agencies operate. It should be emphasized that agencies contribute to the goals of the criminal justice systems, as well as to the service and management systems in the jurisdictions in which they perform their duties.

The present ethical standards in law enforcement shall be reviewed with students. A student who serves any law enforcement capacity (for example, as a cadet or a recruit or as intern, student participant, or researcher) is expected to follow the ethical standards of the profession. (A.A.P.L.E., 1978, pp. 7,8)

In developing a criminal justice program, administrators should recognize the need for cooperation with practitioners and their agencies within the context of acceptable academic practices. Consequently the criminal justice administrator must prevent any direct decision-making involvement by external agencies in matters concerning faculty and curriculum. Others may contribute to decisions and make recommendations, but the final decision must rest with the academic community.

College administrators, working with the law enforcement community,

> must build a relationship over a long period of time, defining problems and working jointly toward solutions. Academics must become intimately familiar with the police and their needs. They should associate directly with a police agency and its personnel. And they must be willing to engage in applied research. The police, on the other hand, must become familiar with the tools and capacities of the academics (Goldstein, 1977, p. 302).

The relationship between academics and practitioners requires a delicate balance which may be difficult to sustain. Nevertheless, the college administrator must protect the criminal justice education program from undue external pressures. As a result, the administration has an obligation to provide guidance and support that will enable a program to prosper.

SUMMARY

L.E.A.A. and its L.E.E.P. programs certainly provided a stimulus to the development of criminal justice education. In accepting federal dollars, college and university administrators also accepted the responsibility to realize the established goals which have yet to be fully met. By delegating to the federal government the authority to plan, implement, and review curricula, university administrators probably yielded a measure of faculty autonomy. L.E.E.P. attracted many inservice students to colleges which frequently had to make major changes to accommodate them. However, statistics indicate that by the late 1970's the effectiveness of L.E.E.P. was waning. Not only had the numbers of L.E.E.P. supported students decreased but the percentages of L.E.E.P. supported individuals within criminal justice programs had also dropped significantly. By 1980, at the time of the Joint Commission student survey, only 24% of the students enrolled in criminal justice courses were being funded by L.E.E.P. In 1981 the L.E.E.P. program was dismantled, but criminal justice higher education had gained acceptance within the academic community.

For the future, college and university administrators must recognize the need for comprehensive planning for criminal justice education. The history of the field is generally a history of personalities, as witnessed in some measure by the various directions that programs have taken. Criminal justice administrators must be involved in both the academic and financial planning of their programs. They must also involve their faculties in the academic process. Finally, they must use the broad resources of the field through involvement and participation in the activities of professional associations and other groups that are examining the frontiers of knowledge in criminal justice education.

Chapter VI
CURRICULUM

At the center of any discussion of academic disciplines is the issue of curricula. Any academic program usually provokes expected controversies over curricula and curriculum development. The Commission was very interested in the development of the undergraduate major within criminal justice and criminology programs.

> The major or concentration, which usually consists of a number of courses in one field or in two or more related fields, is the component of the undergraduate curricula. It is intended to provide students with a body of knowledge, methods of study, and practice appropriate to a subject or subject area. A possible exception to this is the competency based major, which is rooted in outcomes other than in courses and, at least theoretically, may involve no courses at all (*Handbook on Undergraduate Curriculum*, 1978, p.30).

Although several programs exist that are based upon competency measured by "life experience credits," the majority of criminal justice and criminology curricula are traditional in orientation. As Bowen (1977) stated, "Few critics of higher education find curricula rational" (p. 413). Although most educators believe in a concept of a specific curriculum with required and elective courses, individual programs greatly differ, and faculty often disagree about the availability and content of courses. Bowen identifies three broadly philosophical approaches to curriculum development: traditionalist, professionalist, and fusionist (p. 414).

In sharp contrast to their name, traditionalists hold no single, universally accepted "traditional" position and no set of common assumptions beyond a basic philosophical commitment to "defend images of higher education, culture, and personality fashioned largely in the nineteenth century (or earlier)" (Bowen, 1977, p. 414). Traditionalists place great emphasis on the transmission of knowledge through the study of historical development. Although most educators would grant the validity of the traditionalist viewpoint, few would accept it completely. Nevertheless,

> The traditionalist ideal remains the touchstone against which changes of purpose are measured, the icon toward which proponents and rationalizers of educational change must bow, if only perfunctorily (ibid., p. 420).

Contrary to the traditionalists, professionalists place greater emphasis on the utilitarian value of higher education. Their philosophical position, although less unified than that of the traditionalists, nevertheless sets definite educational goals. Carl Kaysen, one of their spokesmen, states, "We should offer some kind of professional training as the central means toward securing the results we seek: the creation of the critical, inquiring, and informed mind" (quoted in Bowen, 1977, p. 421). Kaysen argues that a professionalist approach is consistent with the pragmatic strain in American thought and culture and would therefore be acceptable to a diverse public (ibid., p. 422).

The fusionists, as their name suggests, propose a fusion of traditionalism and professionalism. They acknowledge that the functions of liberal and professional learning at least must continue to coexist in education (Bowen, 1977, p. 423), but between the two poles of thought lies a spectrum of conflicting opinions: What should a curriculum entail? What is its place in a program's organization? How much time, or credit, should be devoted to a particular area of study?

The contemporary debate on curriculum development may

be characterized as fusionist in nature. Few educators today would exclude professional education from the academy. However, many disagree about the place of professional training: should it be part of a university major, or is it to be relegated to vocational and technical schools? When agreement is reached that professional curricula belong in university programs, strong disagreement still occurs about courses and course content. Finally, some argue that professional education belongs only in graduate schools, not in the liberal arts programs of undergraduate colleges.

Although the debate between traditionalist and professionalist is not new, it intensified in the 1960's and 1970's. Many educators view the increased emphasis on professional education--especially on the undergraduate level--as denaturing the liberal component of the educational experience. Bowen has summarized the historical development of the debate over professionalism and traditionalism and argues that it has provided educators with a better, more reasoned understanding of higher education. The controversy over professionalism has, in effect, "demythicized" the ideal of a liberal education while giving traditionalism new relevance to contemporary society:

> In its demythicized form, then, the liberal ideal still constitutes the basic structure or belief (or hope) among critics of American higher education. No longer commanding universal or easy assent, it must be debated constantly, taken as a problem rather than as an unquestioned ideal. But it is a generous, flexible, open-ended vision, subject to enriching radical and conservative revisions of its parts and consistent with a broader range of moods than it once encompassed (Bowen, 1977 p. 427).

When the debate over curriculum was at its peak, the growth of criminal justice programs began as no accident. The decade of the 1960's created an environment in which traditional educational goals were questioned, and practical educational designs changed. Clark Kerr believes that between 1965 and 1970 the most significant change since 1920 occurred in higher education (Kerr, 1979, pp. 15-16). He concludes that during this time, students themselves became the focus of administrative attention and became the very agents of change (see Chart VI-1).

CHART VI-1

The Swings of Academic Change

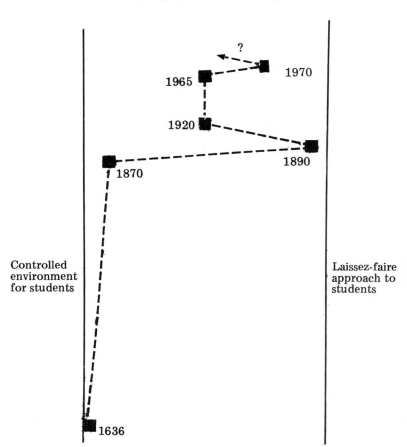

Source: The Administration of Higher Education in an Era of Change and Conflict, "Conflict, Retrenchment, and Reappraisal: The Administration of Higher Education, " 1979, p. 16.

CHART VI-2
CHRONOLOGY OF SIGNIFICANT CURRICULUM
INNOVATIONS, 1900-1973

1. Contemporary Civilization at Columbia University -1919
2. Cooperative Education at Antioch - 1921
3. The Honors Program at Swarthmore - 1921
4. The Cluster College Concept at Claremont College -1925
5. Meiklejohn's Experimental College at the University of Wisconsin - 1927
6. Undergraduate Education at the University of- Chicago - 1928
7. Progressive Education at Bennington - 1932
8. The General College at the University of Minnesota -1932
9. Great Books at St. John's - 1937
10. General Education at Harvard - 1945
11. Post-Sputnik Pressure at Oakland University - 1959
12. Education for Excellence at New College - 1964
13. Tussman's Experimental College Program at the University of California, Berkeley - 1965
14. The Student-Run Free University at Berkeley - 1965
15. Collegiate Education at the University of California, Santa Cruz - 1965
16. An "Early College" at Simon's Rock - 1965
17. Bensalem College at Fordham University - 1967
18. Comprehensive Community College in the Flathead Valley - 1967
19. Curriculum Reform at Brown University - 1969
20. Experimenting at Hampshire College - 1970
21. Awarding Degrees at a Proprietary School: Technical Career Institutes - 1970
22. University Reform through New College at The University of Alabama, Tuscaloosa - 1971
23. Nontraditional Education at Metropolitan State University - 1972
24. Competency-based Education at Sterling College -1972
25. Educational Brokering at the Capital Higher Education Education Service, Inc. pp. 328-417.

Source: *Handbook on Undergraduate Curriculum*, Education Service, Inc. pp. 328-417.

During this period, curricula changed markedly, and one locus of change was the undergraduate major.

> Most colleges (89%) have a major requirement. Such requirements are more common in profes-sional/technical colleges (business, education, engineering, health sciences, and trade/technical) than arts and sciences colleges (96% versus 85%). They are also more common in four-year undergraduate programs than in two-year undergraduate programs (97% versus 48%) *(Handbook on Undergraduate Curriculum,* 1978, p. 31).

Although the number of students has probably not changed significantly, the proportions of students in various fields certainly have. The number of students enrolled in professional or technical courses has increased, thereby reducing the proportion, if not the numbers, of students in liberal arts programs. To understand the nature of curriculum reform and changes an historical perspective may help. The Carnegie Council on Policy Studies in Higher Education's *Publication on Undergraduate Curriculum* outlines significant curriculum innovations that have occurred since 1900 (see Chart VI-2).

These innovations support Kerr's theory that the 1960's was the decade of significant curriculum change because eight innovations are listed for that period. During the 1960's, educators placed greater emphasis on and became sensitive to the student body. They also began emphasizing professional education (Sandeen, 1976, p.47).

Writing about the increase of professional schools, Charles Wegener observed:

> . . . Part of the University idea was to raise the in-tellectual level of the professions by creating profes-sional schools which were an integral part of the University, sharing in and contributing to its in-tellectual ambience, as some sort of guarantee that theory could not degenerate into merely vocational or technical training (Wegener, 1978, p.82).

Wegener's remarks on graduate schools also apply to undergraduate professional programs. A frequent argument made for professional majors in colleges is the need to "upgrade" specific professional occupations. The primary movement to establish criminal justice programs rested on the assumption that higher education would improve the quality of personnel in criminal justice agencies. The Report of the National Advisory Commission on Criminal Justice Standards and Goals recommended:

> Criminal justice system curricula and programs be established by agencies of higher education to unify the body of knowledge in law enforcement, criminology, social science, criminal law, public administration, and corrections, and to serve as a basis for preparing persons to work in the criminal justice system (p.78).

Faculty attitudes toward criminal justice and criminology play a vital role in the formulation and establishment of curricula. The Joint Commission's interest in faculty attitudes, however, necessitated a review of faculty attitudes in other disciplines. In all disciplines, faculty agreement on curricula is rare. The Carnegie Commission Surveys in 1975-76 indicated that a large percentage of faculty felt the need to reform undergraduate curricula at their respective institutions (See Table VI-1). Although 44% of all faculty believe that undergraduate curricula need serious reform, they generally, for whatever reasons, resist change (p. 425). Generally, the nature of institutions with their political and procedural labyrinths, make substantive changes a long and difficult process (see Sandeen, 1976, p. 46). Moreover, external forces--government, the courts, the media, professional associations, and financial donors all influence institutional change and curriculum development (see *Handbook on Undergraduate Curriculum*, p.427). These external forces provide continuing conflicting demands on an institution's programs. In the field of criminal justice, one external force--federal funding--shaped the development of programs. For the 1970's, another external force upon the field was the increasing number of Vietnam veterans whose tuitions were paid primarily by state and federal assistance programs (see Sandeen, 1976, p. 41), channeled through L.E.E.P. and the Veterans Administration (Misner, 1975, p.16).

Another historical influence affecting the increase of criminal justice programs was the move toward vocationalism in higher education (Jencks and Riesman, 1968, pp. 199-201).

Frederick Rudolph notes that after 1900 most colleges had added education programs with a major commitment to train secondary school teachers (p. 215). "If the curriculum moved steadily away from the old subjects toward an explicit and sometimes strident vocationalism," Rudolph writes, "it also succeeded in transferring some of the old purpose and service ideal into new courses and programs" (p.219).

TABLE VI-1
PERCENTAGE OF FACULTY BY CARNEGIE TYPE AGREEING
THAT THE UNDERGRADUATE CURRICULA AT THEIR
INSTITUTIONS ARE IN SERIOUS NEED OF REFORM

Research Universities I	40
Research Universities II	47
Doctorate-Granting Universities I	45
Doctorate-Granting Universities II	50
Comprehensive Universities and Colleges I	48
Comprehensive Universities and Colleges II	52
Liberal Arts College I	36
Liberal Arts College II	43
Two-Year Colleges	40

Source: Handbook on Undergraduate Curricula, 1978, p. 425

The implementation of criminal justice curricula in the 1960's was but one of many additions to established programs of study, but the rapid increase in student interest and demand in criminal justice resulted in a growth surpassing that of other newly accepted programs. Figure VI-1 lists the percentages of professional and technical majors, including enforcement programs, that appeared in the Carnegie Commission catalog study conducted in 1976. In less than a decade these majors were represented in undergraduate curricula.

For Charles Wegener (1978) a curriculum is part of a broad "educational strategy," it is a program that provides the "tools for solving a certain kind of problem." As "that which teaches or educates," a curriculum provides a certain structure to classroom activity. However, Wegener challenges the "dogma common among many academics that curriculum is of little importance, and that teaching is, or that teachers are." Curriculum planning "is a matter of supreme practical importance" (Wegener, p. 139).

Given Wegener's view of the importance of curriculum development, the history of criminal justice education in America can be viewed as a history of curricula. As the field developed from academic sociology and from practical police science, debates over curricula began. With the infusion of federal funds into established criminal justice programs and with public pressure for new programs, many other external forces began to influence the structure and purpose of curricula.

The contemporary debate on curricular issues centers on six historically established positions:

1. Emphasis on the Criminal Justice System. Proponents maintain that curricula have generally been too narrowly and closely linked to police studies or corrections, and that more emphasis needs to be placed on studying the criminal justice system as a whole.

2. Theory vs. "Practical" Studies. Proponents are concerned with the difference between what is termed "theoretically" based curricula or the teaching of theory and general knowledge and what is termed "practical" based curricula, emphasizing the pragmatic demands of an occupation.

3. Administrative and Management Emphasis vs. a Social Science Approach. Proponents who emphasize administrative management maintain that criminal justice studies, not unlike business programs, prepare future managers for the field and should therefore concentrate on administrative training. The

FIGURE VI-1
PERCENTAGE OF DIFFERENT TYPES OF COLLEGES AND
UNIVERSITIES WITH PROFESSIONAL AND TECHNICAL MAJORS

Types of Institutions

Professional and Technical Majors	Research Universities	Doctorate-granting Universities	Comprehensive Universities & Colleges	Liberal Arts Colleges	Community and Junior Colleges
Business	70	93	91	75	93
Education	82	88	93	84	67
Engineering	80	64	29	5	55
Health science	41	50	55	18	63
Forestry	14	10	6	5	27
Home economics	32	52	22	7	32
Auto and aviation repair	5	10	10	2	32
Electronics	7	12	12	0	32
Professional assistant (to doctor, lawyer, or dentist)	7	5	3	2	27
Mortuary science	0	2	3	0	2
Cosmetology	0	0	1	0	12
Law enforcement	11	43	35	13	60
Secretarial science	9	19	32	14	73
Medical	25	55	46	23	25

Source: Handbook on Undergraduate Curriculum, 1978, p. 119.

social scientists stress the need to develop graduates with a thorough understanding of social problems, which is attainable only through strong social science curricula.

4. Practitioners vs. Teachers and Researchers. Although less pronounced at the undergraduate level, proponents are concerned about colleges graduating practitioners or researchers and future teachers.

5. Elimination of Undergraduate Criminal Justice Curricula. A few individuals contend that colleges should remain devoted to general liberal arts education and that criminal justice studies should be offered at the graduate level only.

6. Broadening Criminal Justice Education to Include All Aspects of the Justice System. Proponents would include the study of civil, juvenile, and military justice systems in addition the study of criminal justice.

The explicit or implicit dichotomies in these positions reflect a larger dichotomy in the history of American higher education. As Richard Pearson at the Joint Commissions symposium stated:

> ...the dichotomy that appeared when Charles Eliot introduced elective courses at Harvard eighty years ago. Ever since, the undergraduate curriculum has had to strike a balance between conflicting student needs for "distribution" and for "concentration," and the balance has varied from campus to campus and from time to time, not least because of growing specialization in most fields.
>
> The subsequent history of college attempts to define an appropriate distribution and concentration in the undergraduate curriculum shows clearly that both emphases are essential and that both must be accommodated in the four undergraduate years.

If the history of criminal justice education is the history of curricula, then a detailed examination of that history should help evaluate the present state of the profession and set priorities for the future. That history, moreover, reveals the continuing tensions among departments, academic administrations, faculties, the public, theoreticians and practitioners. As they designed and implemented curricula, three schools—University of California at Berkeley, San Jose State University, and John Jay College of Criminal Justice—served as models in attempting to resolve the continuing tensions that have characterized criminal justice education.

THE BERKELEY CRIMINOLOGY PROGRAM

By 1916, August Vollmer had established a formal relationship with the University of California at Berkeley (Carte, pp. 27-8). By 1933, he had been appointed as a faculty member to the university on a Rockefeller Foundation grant. In cooperation with Herman Adler, Hugh Fuller, and others, Vollmer established a major in criminology. Gene Carte characterized the police curriculum Vollmer designed as "intended to give the student a general education in academic subjects related to the field. It was not meant to be a technical police school within a university setting" (p. 69).

Vollmer's ideal of "university-trained policemen" was to involve instruction, not only in police science but also in public speaking, sociology, psychology, abnormal psychology, and statistics. In formulating his curricular goals, Vollmer consulted with police chiefs, notably O.W. Wilson, to get a broad sense of departmental needs and social purpose. However, Vollmer's plans were slow to be implemented, because his intentions were seldom understood by the university's administration. As a Berkeley memorandum of December, 1944, illustrates, nearly a decade elapsed between Vollmer's initial appointment (1931) and the final, administrative approval for a full-time professor of police administration who was O.W. Wilson, appointed in 1940. (Memorandum on Police Administration and Criminology Program Development, December, 1944).

In 1939 what was to become the School of Criminology made a proposal for a comprehensive program. The recommendations in the proposal provided a framework for many subsequent programs. The proposed, dated November 20, 1939, recommended establishing a Department of Criminology that would offer the following courses:

> *Principles and Problems of Criminology* - The biologic, social, political, economic and psychological factors of crime. A study of the framework of the institutions: police, courts, probation, prison, parole. Theories of the cause, the prevention, the control, and the treatment of the criminal.

Principles of Police Organization and Administration - An introduction to the principles of police organization and administration, discussion of police statistics, criminal identification and investigation, and educational methods for combating crime and vice and controlling traffic.

Investigation and Identification - Principles of criminal investigation and personal identification including a discussion of fingerprinting.

Public Safety - An orientation course covering the causes of traffic accidents and congestion; the approach through engineering, education, and enforcement. Surveys, engineering factors, pedestrian control, throughways, one-way streets, signal control, organization for traffic control. Administrative problems, public education and driver training enforcement and the courts.

Legal Relations Involved in Criminology - History of criminal law, relation to civil law, penal code, arrest, searches and seizures, evidence, special classes of persons.

Criminological Microscopy - Microscopic methods in criminal investigation. The identification and individualization of material of criminological significance, including poisons, paint, animal and vegetable fibers, physiological fluids, papers, inks, and residues.

Forensic Medicine and Toxicology - Study of wounds and fractures from point of view of cause. Physiological reactions to poisons.

Criminal Psychology and Psychiatry - The interpretation of the behavior of criminals, the causes of neurotic disturbances.

Special Study for Advanced Undergraduates - Problem course for advanced students interested in any aspect of criminology.

Research in Criminology - Graduate research in
methods of the criminal investigator and in problems related to the field of criminology.

Graduate Seminar in Criminology - (variable credit),
I and II. (This is the same as Political Science 267,
except that the scope will be broadened to include
forensic science).

Vollmer's curriculum reveals that criminal justice studies
were considered interdisciplinary fields and that the training
of a "criminologist" required a broad background in
undergraduate forensic studies.

Vollmer's efforts apparently faltered. Between 1941 and
1943, his program at Berkeley was called the Bureau of
Criminology. When, on September 20, 1940, O.W. Wilson re-
quested an increase of $18,900 in the budget to implement
Vollmer's proposals, he was given a budgetary increase of
$10,000.

In 1942, Vollmer wrote optimistically in the *Journal of
Criminal Law*, "The teaching of police subjects has at last
become respectable enough to be included in the offerings of institutions of higher learning" (p. 200). Vollmer was a professor
of police science and administration at the State College of
Washington, and was no doubt unaware of the uncertain
future of his program at Berkeley.

Vollmer's program played a major role in framing the
historical development of the criminal justice field, and his curriculum proposals became guide-posts for many future
criminology programs. Unfortunately, the history of the
Berkeley program includes the frequent conflicts between
criminology and criminal justice educators and the university
administrations. From Wilson's appointment in 1940 to the
school's final closing in the 1970's, the history of the Berkeley
program is a history of administrative reports and studies
questioning the program's proper function within the university. The program's survival was also impeded by its relationship to the state; although the School of Criminology was
originally approved by the California legislature, several years
elasped before it actually began to function.

Perhaps the most important document concerning the
school's history and development is the so-called Cline Report,
submitted to the Berkeley chancellor in 1959. The report clearly recognized demonstrable problems with an organized School

of Criminology and recommended discontinuing the program of criminology as well as the School. The report considered "this kind of training in criminology" to be the prerogative of state colleges, not that of large universities. Nonetheless, others disagreed:

> That where there is evidence of demand for training in specific areas at the graduate level, departments whose subjects are susceptible of application to the problem of crime should be encouraged to offer appropriate courses to their graduate majors. (Cited in *Reply by the School of Criminology to the Cline Report*, August 20, 1959, p. 4).

However, the Cline Report left open the possibility of a future program in criminology:

> If at some time in the future the scientific foundations of this field are more clearly defined and crystalized, the university may well consider reintroducing training in research in criminology (ibid., p. 4).

The Cline Report essentially based its recommendations on two premises: 1. that training in criminology belonged in a technical or vocational program at the state college level rather than in an academic one; and 2. that the state of the criminal justice field had not yet reached a level which justified its inclusion in a university department. In the *Reply by the School of Criminology to the Cline Report*, the faculty proposed many of the arguments that would justify the establishment of many academic criminal justice programs in this country.

The faculty acknowledged that the primary focus of their program was practical rather than theoretical, but they argued for criminology's status as a discipline, "with a large 'common body of knowledge' " (*Reply*, p. 21). To the Cline Report's contention that the field was undefined, the faculty replied, "Criminology is a rapidly growing and increasingly well-integrated discipline" (p. 21), and "more than a hundred graduates have been appointed to positions in various police and federal services" (p. 26). However, the faculty admitted, "Most of these young graduates have not had time to rise to administrative positions, but a substantial number have been promoted to positions of increased responsibility" (p. 26). Concerning their unique criminalistics program, the faculty claimed that theirs was "the only school offering a complete program in the field, and it is widely recognized as the source of the best trained criminalists available" (p. 27).

A 1960 report by a committee on the re-organization of the School of Criminology's curriculum made several recommendations for change. Against the stigma of vocationalism, the committee attempted to reorient the curriculum to treat the social and psychological aspects of criminology. They stated, "These areas are essential in the scholarly consideration of the broad problem of crime and law enforcement and constitute the areas in which fundamental research should be conducted" (from a confidential memorandum to Chancellor Glen T. Seaborg, November 11, 1960, from the committee). The committee sought to focus on research and the scholarly nature of criminology. They recommended expanding instruction on the legal aspects of criminology, and they sought to de-emphasize instruction in the routine aspects of criminalistics, while recommending that the criminalistics program be retained. Their report highlighted the tensions between faculty and administration in no uncertain terms:

> We are not recommending any changes in the program of courses as presented by Professor Kirk . . . Subsequently, after the new dean has had the opportunity to familiarize himself with the criminalistics program and to study it in detail, the criminalistics program should be reviewed by a faculty committee with the assistance of the new dean.

The committee's tone clearly defined the conflicts between the ideals of programs such as criminology and the realities of administrative approval. The committee stressed again and again that their recommendations to "streamline" the program by eliminating and combining courses was not a repudiation of the field's uniqueness but rather a commitment to interdisciplinary objectives.

By the mid-1970's the School of Criminology was closed, and no new students were admitted. Ironically, at this time several new courses in legal studies were offered, some taught by the "old" criminology faculty and some strikingly similar to courses in the criminology program. In 1980 an undergraduate major in legal studies appeared, and criminalistic courses continue to be offered within the College of Public Health. Other universities have initiated criminology programs. In 1929, the University of Chicago established a police science program that functioned only three years. Nonetheless, the program was, according to Foster, "The first degree program in crime related studies to be housed in political science in a university and represents the first effort to place technical police training courses in a regular undergraduate curriculum" (Foster, p.32).

SAN JOSE STATE AND POLICE ADMINISTRATION

The program in criminal justice at San Jose State University--then known as San Jose State Teacher's College--began in 1930 as a two-year technical training program in police administration (Kuykendall and Hernandez, 1975). Kuykendall and Hernandez analyzed the program's development from its inception until 1975. Their findings indicate a shifting emphasis in the curriculum from police administration to a broad inclusive approach.

Between 1930 and 1935, almost the entire curriculum was concerned with law enforcement. No attention was paid to social deviance or corrections. Between 1970 and 1975 a dramatic shift took place. Over half of the curriculum was devoted to the "criminal justice system; 25% was devoted to law enforcement; and 18% of the curriculum was concerned with corrections. Between 1930 and 1970, the curriculum was

TABLE VI-2
SAN JOSE STATE UNIVERSITY
PERCENT OF CURRICULUM BY
SUBJECT AREA AND TIME PERIOD

Subject Area	1930-35	1935-42[al]	Time Periods 1946-64	1964-70	1970-75
Social deviance	0	0	0[bl]	0[cl]	0	0
Law enforcement	93	97	81	86	88	25
Corrections	0	0	12	7	7	18
System	7	3	7	7	5	57

[al] Based on four-year degree.
[bl] Based on academic year 1955-56.
[cl] Based on academic year 1962-63.

Source: Kuykendall, Jack and Armand Hernandez, "Undergraduate Justice System and Training at San Jose State University: An Historical Perspective." *Journal of Criminal Justice.* Vol. 3, 1975.

relatively stable with law enforcement's share of courses declining slightly from 93% to 88%. The abrupt decline for law enforcement occurred between 1970 and 1975, from an 88% to a 25% share of the curriculum. Table VI-2 illustrates some of the historical changes in the San Jose curriculum.

JOHN JAY COLLEGE—POLICE SCIENCE MODEL

One of the most extensive and influential curricula for criminology and criminal justice was the police science model curriculum (Figure VI-2) developed in the late 1960's and early 1970's at John Jay College of Criminal Justice. Leo Loughrey and Herbert Friese, writing in the *Journal of Criminal Law, Criminology and Police Science* in 1969, proposed a curriculum for police science programs which, in their view, had widespread applicability (pp. 265-271).

Loughrey and Friese wanted to determine which courses had "common value to both types of students, that is to say, those courses which are of equal use to our professional police officer and to our recent high school graduate" (p. 266). They considered "communication skills" basically important:

> In police work, a man must be able to express himself clearly and make himself understood. He must also have the capacity to understand exactly what it is that somebody is saying. Hence, for all students, communication skills are developed by a variety of courses: English, Speech, Literature, Music, Philosophy, Religion, and Foreign Languages. Although none of these directly relates to Police Science, a man will function more effectively as a police officer after becoming more proficient in them (p. 266).

Figure VI-2
FOUR YEAR CORE AT JOHN JAY COLLEGE

NOTE: Core courses at John Jay are designated by department and course number (i.e. English 101). However, abbreviated titles are used here for clarity.

Liberal Arts-prescribed for all students

A.   Humanities
      English Composition (2 terms)

Advanced Exposition
Fundamentals of Speech
Discussion, Conference, and Public Speaking
Western Literature (2 terms)
History of Civilization (2 terms)
Art
Drama
American History
Music
Moral Philosophy
Comparative Religion
Advanced Spanish
Spanish
> Students may satisfy the foreign language require-
> ment for the degree by passing the fourth term
> course in Spanish (202 or a higher course), or by
> passing a proficiency examination in Spanish, or by
> establishing proficiency in speaking, reading, and
> writing another foreign language, but will not be
> given college credit except for courses taken.
> Students will be placed in the appropriate Spanish
> course on the basis of two terms of Spanish in high
> school equalling one term of college Spanish.

B. Science and Mathematics
Mathematics (2 terms)
College Science (2 terms)

C. Social Sciences
General Psychology
Introductory Sociology
Introduction to Anthropology
American Government
Principles of Economics

D. Other Required Courses
American System of Criminal Justice (2 terms)
College Colloquium (an inter-disciplinary seminar)

To the four-year core the following are added:
Courses in the Major Field of Study--Police Science
> This major is intended for the student wishing the max-
> imum concentration of courses in professional police
> work. Courses must be selected from the groups (each
> course is 3 credits):

A.   Pol. Sci. 204-The Patrol Function
      Pol. Sci. 205-The Traffic Control Function
      Pol. Sci. 207-The Investigative Function

B.   Pol. Sci. 201-Police Organization and Management
      Pol. Sci. 301-Police Administration
      Pol. Sci. 401-Police Problems (required)

C.   Law 201-Law of Evidence
      Law 204-Criminal Law of New York
      Law 301-The Nature and Function of Legal Systems
      Law 401-Problems of Constitutional Development

D.   Pol. Sci. 309-Comparative Police Systems
      Pol. Sci. 310-Federal Police Systems in the U.S.
      Pol. Sci. 405-Organized Crime in America
      Pol. Sci. 313-Crime Investigation Laboratory
      Pol. Sci. 314-Crime Scene Laboratory
      Pol. Sci. 303-Police Personnel Administration
      Pol. Sci. 308-Current Problems in Traffic Control
      Pol. Sci. 306-Police Work with Juveniles or any course
        in Groups A,B,D, (above)
      Govt. 103-Municipal and State Government
      Govt. 201-Government and Administration of New York
      City
      Govt. 301-Public Administration
      Govt. 305-Comparative Government
      Govt. 403-Problems of Civil Rights and Civil Liberties
      Psych 205-Adolescent Psychology
      Psych 301-Social Psychology
      Soc. 203-Criminology
      Soc. 205-Juvenile Delinquency
      Soc. 401-Problems of Minority Groups

Free Electives
      Credits beyond those accounted for in the preceding
      groups needed to make up a total of 128 credits for the
      B.S. degree may be freely elected from the entire list of-
      fered by the College, except that no more than one-half
      may be in the same subject.

Source: Leo C. Loughrey and Herbert C. Friese, Jr., "Curriculum Development for a Police Science Program." *Journal
of Criminal Law, Criminology and Police Science,* Vol. 60, No.
2, 1969.

Donald H. Riddle, who served as chairman of the curriculum committee at John Jay, wrote about using vocational training to develop what he called a "vision" and understanding of the large issues confronting police work. Training in sociology, psychology, and anthropology would give a future police officer a necessary "thorough understanding of the man in society, of the nature and development of social institutions, and of the enormous variety in human behavior" (Riddle, 1977, p. 10). "If the policeman is to understand and question his place in the center of social conflict in the modern world," Riddle added, "he must possess a comprehension of 'social phenomena and human behavior.'" Moreover, "a knowledge of class structure, of the sociology of race relations, and of sociological theory are almost essential if one is to understand the social forces at work in American society today" (p. 11).

The John Jay program from its inception had a clearly defined set of philosophical commitments through which it structured course curricula. By 1980, a John Jay study (Pearson, et. al., 1980, p.34) of criminal justice education identified three broad approaches to the organization of criminal justice programs:

> *Technical-Vocational.* A program of this type emphasized the development of competency in those specific skills deemed essential for criminal justice practitioners effectively to realize the mission. Allegedly, the vast majority of two-year programs are technical-vocational. They are collegiate programs and not agency training academy offerings. Although the same institution may sponsor a training program, it appears to be normal practice for it to be separate from the academic component, although it is closely related.

> *Professional-Managerial.* Heretofore, those discussing criminal justice education tended to use the labels "technical" and "professional" interchangeably. The researchers felt that the labeling was confusing and concealed the fact that, although programs emphasizing the technical-vocational and professional-managerial philosophies both dealt with the "real world" of criminal justice, the focus and concern of each were substantially different. A professional-managerial program emphasizes

TABLE VI-3
TECHNICAL-VOCATIONAL OFFERINGS IN
CRIMINAL JUSTICE EDUCATION
(By Percentage)

Note: The John Jay researchers presented results based on
respondents' self-assessment of their own programs, but the
National Planning Association calculated its figures on the
basis of the proportion of technical courses as opposed to the
total criminal justice offerings.

Institutions	Proportion of Technical-Vocational Offerings
All Institutions	
National Planning Association (L.E.A.A.) [al]	14.6
John Jay	15.5
Two-year Colleges	
National Planning Association (L.E.A.A.) [al]	24.4
John Jay	27.8
Four-year Colleges (and Universities)	
National Planning Association (L.E.A.A.) [bl]	8.8 (8.5)
John Jay	9.8

[al] National Planning Association: A nationwide survey of law
enforcement criminal justice personnel needs and resources:
interim report (prepared for the National Institute of Law
Enforcement and Criminal Justice/Law Enforcement Assistance
Administration/U.S. Department of Justice, June 30, 1976).

[bl] Ibid. (In addition, the parenthetical entry is for university level
programs, a category not readily available from the John Jay data.)

Source: Pearson, et al. *Criminal Justice Education: The End of The
Beginning*, 1980, pp. 79-80.

management and administrative skill and a broad
overview of those areas with which senior agency
administrators are involved. This model is
presented in a business administration/public administration" context and tends not to include
broad social science and humanities courses.

Humanistic-Social. The goal of a program of this
type is the development of the "whole person" who
is able to understand the problems of society and
their milieu. The roles of criminal justice administration in society and of the criminal justice
practitioner as public servant are emphasized. The
program is apt to de-emphasize the agency-specific
perspective as well as the managerial point of view
(p. 35-36).

In addition to outlining the various types of existing programs, the John Jay study commented on contemporary
perceptions of the criminal justice field. The study noted, "A
considerable consensus appears to have developed about some
of the basic issues of curriculum development." Moreover,
"Criminal justice education appears to be in the process of being assimilated into the traditional college environment" (p.
41). What the John Jay study recognizes is a "consensus" to
move away from technical-vocational and professional-
managerial philosophies and move toward a humanistic-social
model (see also Brandstatter and Hoover, 1976). Challenging
public expectations, the data in Table VI-3 reveal that the
percentage of technical-vocational programs is not as great as
might be suspected.
   An examination of the curriculum developments at
Berkeley, San Jose, and John Jay indicate a broad understanding of the relationships between faculties and administrations and between philosophical and practical approaches to
curriculum development. Peter Lejins, one of the pioneers
described his premises for post secondary criminology and
criminal justice education. Lejins considered "social action"
against crime to be no different than social action against
other problems in the community. Social action would "be ap-
propriately based on the accumulation of the specific
knowledge and skills gradually developed in a society's deal-
ings with these problems" (p. 28). The accumulation of
"specific knowledge," for Lejins, would be accomplished by

FIGURE VI-3
LEJIN'S SUGGESTED UNDERGRADUATE
CURRICULUM IN CRIMINOLOGY AND CORRECTIONS
1968

1. A general introductory survey course in criminology.

2. A general introductory survey course in juvenile delinquency.

3. An introductory course in institutional treatment.

4. An introductory course in community-based treatment including probation and parole.

5. A survey course in prevention.

6. A field training course or placement with a correctional or preventive institution or agency.

> The above group of courses would provide an appropriate and at the same time the maximum possible concentration for an undergraduate student.

> This criminology and corrections course would be combined with three additional elements:

1. Undergraduate core courses in sociology.

2. Introductory sociology and such areas as abnormal psychology, tests and measurements, and some developmental psychology.

3. The general university and/or liberal arts requirements.

Source: "Content of the Curriculum and Its Relevance for Correctional Programs," *Joint Commission on Correctional Manpower of Training, Criminology and Corrections; A Study of the Issues,* 1968, p.54. *Correctional Association,* 1972, p.54.

"special personnel imbued by means of special education with the available specific knowledge." For Lejins, corrections means "the removal of the causes, reasons, motivations, or factors that are responsible for the criminal or delinquent behavior" (p. 29). Because Lejins adopts a method of social psychology in calling corrections a form of "behavior modification," the training of professionals must, like that of social scientists, be through "college or university level education" (p.29). Summarizing his perspective, Lejins writes:

> I begin with the premise or conclusion that the proper basis for effective action against crime and delinquency is university trained personnel to whom has been imparted the existing body of knowledge in interpreting crime and delinquency as well as in removing the causes thereof and to whom have also been imparted the corresponding skills for modification of this behavior (p. 29).

Lejin's conception (Figure VI-3) of a criminology curriculum is not unlike a program of study for any academic degree, be it "chemistry, botany, physics, engineering, history, psychology, etc." (Lejins, p. 49).

Like Lejins, Vernon Fox (1968, p. 57) quickly recognized the problem of integrating practical training with the study of theory within a university environment. Although admitting the importance of the junior college in providing police science training, Fox nevertheless argued that "The curriculum must be built with concern for university level scholarship" (p. 64). Fox recognized the hybrid nature of such curricula and the confusion that arose when junior college training was implemented at the university level. To avoid confusion, Fox argued that the university must restrict itself to theoretical considerations. The university curriculum "must emphasize the theory and practice of social control as a psychological, social, and legal problem of dysfunction in modern society" (p. 64).

The debate over theory vs. practice has always preoccupied writers on criminal justice, and the debate has not ended. Faculties with strong vocational traditions naturally establish curricula with strong practical emphases. Departments with a social science bias usually stress theory and methodology in

teaching their students. During the 1960's, the debate took on
its sharpest contours. Donald Riddle has noted:

> . . . In the early sixties, at the time of the boom in
> "police science" or "police administration" educa-
> tion, there is a strong tendency to adopt courses
> which followed readily identifiable topics in the
> police training curriculum or were recognized ac-
> tivities in the police service. Courses on patrol, in-
> vestigations, report writing, etc. were the rule
> rather than the exception, and the tendency even
> carried to providing special applied courses in some
> of the allied fields such as "psychology for police"
> (Riddle, 1977).

As Charles Tenney noted, only when the outside personnel
were employed to reevaluate and redesign curricula were programs placed on a "distinctly demanding level" different from
mere technical courses (*Higher Education Programs in Law
Enforcement and Criminal Justice,* p. 24). The 1960s and 1970s
brought a significant reduction in inservice students and a cor-
responding increase in preservice students. Given these
changes, any assessment of curricula and any proposals for
reform must consider a different student body--one concerned
not with sharpening on-the-job skills but rather one concerned
with the intellectual preparation for a career.

In the 1970's the Police Foundation's National Advisory
Commission on Higher Education for Police Officers reviewed
the general quality of education and found it wanting (Sherman, 1978, p. 61). "The curriculum in most programs does little more than provide a theoretical training in basic police
skills. Unless the prevailing curriculum is changed, it will not
succeed in educating the police institution for change" (Sherman, 1978, p. 61). Moreover, the Commission found an "intellectual aridity of this curriculum," and realized that the
"packaging" of programs in accordance with the guidelines in
an Office of Education pamphlet belied a "rather low level of
complexity" (p. 80).

The findings of the Police Foundation Study supported a
general view that many criminal justice curricula are oriented
towards law enforcement or police. If the student body was
comprised of an increasing number of preservice students,
then the curricula must change. The Commission noted, "The
primary argument for a professional education curriculum for

police officers is that . . .it will help to professionalize the police" (p. 76). What would constitute a professional education curriculum to administrators and faculty who were debating about the kinds of programs they could provide? Many programs offer general training as well as specialization in areas like corrections and the judiciary (see Table VI-4). A need exists to clarify the issues in these debates and to find a reasonable resolution within the confusion and polemics of different studies and approaches.

Many voices are still raised in these debates. On an undergraduate level, liberal arts and "liberal" criminal justice curricula seem at odds with vocational programs of training (see Sherman, pp. 67-86; Goldstein, 1977; Myren, 1970; Misner, 1977; Bittner, 1970; Riddle, 1975; Pearson, 1980; Strecher, 1977). As Simpson states, "It is very possible that the major cause of debate lies in the different policies and objectives sought by educational programs at the various levels" (1979, p. 67). Referring to the Police Foundation study, Simpson notes:

> . . . The National Advisory Commission on Higher Education for Police Officers has resurrected a model of criminal justice education that has not been popular in recent years. In its 1978 report, the Commission subscribes to a quite traditional version of the social sciences/liberal arts model and suggests that the focus of programs in this area should be on moral issues and the results of social science research (p. 73).

However, strong evidence exists to indicate that criminal justice curricula are changing. Myren states, "There seems to be little doubt either that more crime related programs are being developed at educational institutions in the United States every year, or that these tend to be social science/humanistic in their orientation and criminal justice in their label" (1979, p. 29). Many programs called "criminology" seem strikingly similar to those called "criminal justice." Although Brantingham (1972) argued that the two goals of undergraduate training in criminology should be preparation for graduate work and preparation for professional practice, the John Jay study described a shift in both name and content from programs emphasizing practical preparation to those stressing theoretical understanding. Richard Myren's plea for clarity of

TABLE VI-4

FREQUENCY OF DEGREE OFFERING BY INSTITUTION TYPE FOR INSTITUTIONS PARTICIPATING IN THE LAW ENFORCEMENT EDUCATION PROGRAM FOR THE ACADEMIC YEAR 1972-1973

Degree Title	Institution Type N=683			
	University N=158	Other Four Year N=125	Two Year N=400	Total[a] N=683
Law Enforcement/Police Science/ Police Administration	88 (33.7)	54 (34.2)	337 (67.7)	479 (52.3)
Forensic Science/Criminalistics	8 (3.1)	3 (1.9)	5 (1.0)	16 (1.7)
Security	0 (0)	1 (.6)	1 (.2)	2 (.2)
Judicial Management/Court Administration	2 (.7)	2 (1.3)	0 (0)	4 (.4)
Corrections/Correctional Admn./ Probation & Parole	32 (12.3)	18 (11.4)	74 (14.9)	124 (13.6)
Social Welfare/Social Work	7 (2.7)	4 (2.5)	1 (.2)	12 (1.3)
Criminal Justice/Criminal Justice Administration	47 (18.1)	36 (22.8)	27 (5.4)	110 (12.1)
Administration of Justice	8 (3.1)	7 (4.4)	15 (3.0)	30 (3.3)
Criminology	13 (5.0)	7 (4.4)	9 (1.8)	29 (3.2)
Sociology/Anthropology	12 (4.6)	5 (3.2)	0 (0)	17 (1.8)
Psychology	1 (.3)	1 (.6)	0 (0)	2 (.2)
Behavorial Science	1 (.3)	4 (2.5)	1 (.2)	6 (.6)
Public Administration	4 (1.5)	0 (0)	1 (.2)	5 (.5)
Other	38 (14.6)	16 (102)	27 (5.4)	81 (8.9)
TOTAL	261 (100)	158 (100)	498 (100)	917 (100)

[a]The numbers in this column are row totals while the percentage refers to column totals

Source: Foster, James Price, "A Descriptive Analysis of Crime-Related Programs in Higher Education," The Florida State University, 1974.

nomenclature only complicates the field further:

> It is time that we move on, that we not discard
> criminal justice as a valid field of study, but that we
> recognize it as only one justice system within a
> matrix of justice systems, which range from the for-
> mal juvenile, civil, and military systems to the infor-
> mal justice systems that exist in our homes, schools,
> and work places (1980, p.2)

Myren would advocate the term "justiciology" for this "new" academic discipline.

From the confusion concerning curricula, nomenclature, and personal and professional bias, some irrefutable standards do emerge and contribute to a basic curriculum. In a profession beset by debate, much of the professoriate appear to agree on the importance of including certain courses or areas of study in the curricula.

Research conducted by Gordon Misner (1979) indicated that a general agreement exists among criminal justice academics that an undergraduate curriculum should consist of the following eight courses (Pearson, et al., p. 181):

1. Introduction to Criminal Justice
2. Criminology
3. Criminal Law
4. Criminal Procedure
5. Juvenile Delinquency
6. Elementary Statistics
7. The Judicial Process
8. The Correctional Process

Misner's study asked respondents to select course titles rather than course descriptions, but as Misner states, a high level of agreement occurred on the eight courses, and agreement also was found that a criminal investigation course ranked thir-teenth, of those presented, whereas a course in statistics rank-ed sixth (p.181).

Attempts to study and recommend curricula are subject to uncontrollable variables. From institution to institution, the quality and commitment of faculty will vary; the structure of semesters or quarters in the school year will differ; library resources and text selection will be unrelated. Nevertheless, at the undergraduate level, agreement exists on the existence of a body of knowledge with which the student should be familiar. That "core" of material may be interdisciplinary in origin, or it may be drawn from research and theory (Riddle, 1975, pp. 1-2). Whether in the form of introductory coursework or directed independent study, this body of knowledge may be taught and learned through a core curriculum. The Joint Commission has found widespread support for a broadly based core curriculum, rather than for a narrowly focused set of courses (Culbertson and Carr, 1981).

The establishment of a core curriculum does not, however, necessitate stagnation. Within the core, individual courses should be constantly revised to incorporate rapidly growing research findings. Papers in professional journals are beginning to express a need to move away from vocational programs, except when they are part of a technical two-year course. However, many universities are gradually changing standards and will not be accepting any vocational courses for transfer credit (Swank, 1975; Marsh and Stickler, 1972; Meadows, 1978; Hoover and Lund, 1977). Sherman advocated the possibility of attracting "students to a high quality program without treating college credits for police training and life experience as free giveaways or marketing devices" (Sherman, 1978 p. 114). In the search for academic standards, institutions should award "life experience credits" only after a careful case-by-case review, adhering to standard accreditation procedures (Sherman, p. 115).

Although a general consensus seems to exist on the purpose of a two-year program--to "achieve a planned academic balance" (Stinchcomb, 1976, p. 21), the Joint Commission found that at four-year institutions the attitudes and desires of students contributed to curricular confusion and departmental indirection. The Joint Commission learned from 1625 student responses that only 398 (less than 25%) reported completing a course in research methods, although 70% of the group were at least sophomores and 40% were at least juniors. More troubling was the admission that 45% indicated that they did not plan to take a research methods course, and 17% indicated that such a course was unavailable to them. Only 23% had completed a statistics course, and of those who had not, 53% never planned to take a course in statistics.

Faced with these student course preferences, the Joint Commission feels that faculties should actively encourage undergraduates to take courses in research methods and statistics. Faculty should also design curricula that would expose the criminal justice major to these courses in an effective and stimulating way.

The Joint Commission staff was interested in the types and numbers of courses taken by criminal justice students, because that information would provide some objective data on the level of student interest and enrollment in specific completed courses (see Table VI-5).

TABLE VI-5
NUMBER OF COURSES TAKEN BY UNDERGRADUATE
CRIMINAL JUSTICE STUDENTS IN SPECIFIC AREAS

	No. of Courses					
	1	2	3	4	5 or more	0
		No. of Students Enrolled				
Humanities	329	324	264	160	201	337
Natural Science	308	392	303	165	173	269
Social Science	153	233	281	262	570	123
English	274	496	290	214	168	165
Administration of justice	465	278	157	53	65	225
Behavorial (criminology, juvenile delinquency, deviance, etc.)	335	256	150	48	38	340
Corrections	361	159	52	21	9	497
Courts	316	114	35	17	3	559
Law	314	195	77	34	21	465
Law enforcement	337	143	56	29	64	471
Private security	116	34	8	2	5	809

The Commission realized that, to some degree at least, curriculum offerings are determined by the student body. Invariably, student demand or apathy creates the need for or elimination of various courses. The result may be a succession of courses tailored to individual student needs and with little philosophical or pedagogical continuity. The Commission attempted to determine student perceptions of course value from the standpoint of career objectives. Although reflecting a universal distaste for statistics, the data in Table VI-6 do reveal a strong student bias in favor of courses with a practical emphasis.

TABLE VI-6
STUDENT PERCEPTIONS OF THE VALUE OF
COURSES IN TERMS OF THEIR CAREER
OBJECTIVES ON A SCALE OF 1-10

Courses	Not at All Valuable 1...	5	6	Very Valuable 7	8	9	10
Criminology				x			
Criminal law					x		
Criminal procedure				x			
Deviant behavior				x			
Juvenile deliquency					x		
Statistics			x				
Judicial process				x			
Introduction to corrections			x				
Correctional counseling				x			
Probation and parole			x				
Correctional administration			x				
Introduction to law enforcement				x			
Police community relations					x		
Police organization and management				x			
Rules of evidence					x		
Criminal investigation					x		
Research methods				x			

In addition to examining student views of courses, the Commission supported a project that attempted to review course syllabi in an effort to assess course content (Culbertson and Carr, 1980). As a document that formally specifies the general content and explicit organization of a course, a syllabus provides insight into the pedagogical approaches used to present material. A review of syllabi, then, should indicate not only what courses are being offered in criminal justice programs but also how they fit into a curriculum. Table VI-7 illustrates the ten most "popular" courses identified by Culbertson and Carr in this survey of criminal justice programs.

TABLE VI-7
RANK ORDER OF MAJOR COURSE AREAS

Note: The areas of research methods, judicial, and systems approaches were not ranked among the top ten course areas for two-year institutions. In some instances determination of the origin of the course syllabus was impossible. These syllabi were included under "All Institutions."

Rank	All Institutions Course Area	N	4-Year Institutions Course Area	N	2-Year Institutions Course Area	N
1	General and Introduction	347	General and Introduction	206	General and Introduction	75
2	Police	126	Corrections	60	Police	51
3	Law	103	Police	55	Law	27
4	Corrections	92	Law	52	Investigation	18
5	Investigation	34	Investigation	13	Corrections	12
6	Forensic sciences	18	Research methods	13	Forensic sciences	6
7	Research methods	14	Forensic sciences	10	Security and Public Safety	6
8	Security and Public Safety	13	Judicial	8		
9	Judicial	10	Security and Public Safety	7		
10	Systems Approaches	2	Systems Approaches	2		

Source: Culbertson, Robert and Adam F. Carr. Syllabus Design and Construction in Criminal Justice Education, 1980.

Using a model developed by Misner, Culbertson and Carr also constructed a ranking of individual courses at two and four-year colleges. With the exception of two-year colleges and one or two specific courses, Culbertson and Carr's findings parallel those of Misner.

Criminal justice curricula indicate virtually no concern with the ethical aspects of working within the criminal justice system. Two imperatives for the general study of value choices and ethical problems appear in the literature. Sherman (1978, p.88) identifies "competing value systems" at work in all aspects of law enforcement. They transcend the everyday problems of bribe-taking, for example, but raise fundamental questions about the nature of corrections and justice itself. Students must be aware of the applied ethical dilemmas of police work (Sherman, 1978, p.89) as well as the abstract moral problems inherent in any system of justice. A second imperative concerns a code of ethics for criminal justice educators themselves. Reed Adams has noted:

> Establishing a code of ethics for the behavior of law enforcement officers and some other practitioners of social control has been attempted. No code has yet been developed to apply to the behavior of professional individuals in the field of academic criminal justice (Adams, 1976, p.308).

All professions have a code of ethics, Adams states, but not criminal justice. A code of ethics is a need not only for faculty but for students, especially those graduate students who wish to teach in a criminal justice program. Ethics is a problem for both the future agency practitioner and the would-be professor; it should be considered as a course topic in future curricula.

SUMMARY COMMENTS

Although a wide range of course offerings in the criminal justice field exists, educators generally agree about the basic components of a core curriculum. The consensus includes a recognition of the interdisciplinary nature of the field, the necessity of providing liberal education within the context of a criminal justice major, and the need for specific instruction in research methods and statistics.

The Joint Commission recognizes that contemporary problems with curricula are perhaps characteristic of the development of the criminal justice field. The field grew too quickly,
frequently without benefit of an adequate literature and sufficient research. Historically external forces--university administrations, students, government funding restrictions--
probably affected curriculum design and internal faculty decisions. If criminal justice is to gain "respectability" from the
academy and support of the public, it must establish a certain
identity. That identity can be established by implementing a
core curriculum that will have lasting validity with this country's institutions of higher education. Although admitting to
the possibility of individual variation in courses, the Commission stresses the need for general standards and norms against
which those variations can be evaluated.

Chapter VII

FACULTY

Perhaps no question has sparked so much debate in criminal justice agencies and universities as that of who should educate criminal justice personnel. Perhaps in no other field is this question so difficult to answer or is the need to find an answer so great. Since Vollmer, the debate has been about teachers with education or teachers with experience; should agencies, particularly police and corrections, train their own personnel, or should educators teach students to become fully developed individuals while preparing them for criminal justice careers?

Criminal justice may be unique among professional academic fields for its lack of a body of knowledge and literature. More than in schools of law or medicine, the faculty in criminology and criminal justice programs establish the content of their courses. By their textbook selections, course syllabi, sequences of study, and admission and promotion practices, a criminal justice faculty may provide a unique educational experience. As the Carnegie Foundation stated, "Once the faculty is in place, the catalog has largely been written" (Carnegie Foundation, 1977, pp. 8-9; quoted in Sherman, 1978, p. 131).

Because of the importance of faculty in criminal justice, the Joint Commission sought to evaluate faculty quality, status, and self-perceptions to make its recommendations. Several studies of faculty already existed: The National Manpower

Survey of 1976, the Misner study of 1978, and the John Jay study of 1980 as well as accounts in Sherman (1978), Felkenes (1980), and DeZee (1980). In undertaking its study, however, the Joint Commission had two objectives: 1. The Commission wanted to avoid the methodological pitfalls and outdated material of earlier reports, and 2. wanted to address the frequently discussed question of faculty quality. The Joint Commission considered the quality of both full-time and part-time faculty and sought to establish their relative importance in degree granting programs. With a mandate to develop standards, the Joint Commission tried to assess accurately the composition of the criminal justice education profession as a necessary prerequisite to assessing the quality of the field.

The first and most striking characteristic of criminal justice faculty is their apparent youth. As Tables VII-1 and VII-2 reveal, half of them are under forty years of age, and nine-tenths are white and male. Young faculty can affect the quality of the field, bringing to it neither a lifetime experience of work in an agency nor thorough academic preparation. Moreover, any observations on the youthfulness of faculty must be qualified by the fact that among full-time faculty approximately 50% are tenured. Of those who are not tenured, 74.2% considered themselves to be eligible for tenure or on "tenure track." Table VII-3 indicates that among those eligible for tenure, nearly half (49%) have held their positions for less than five years. These statistics indicate that, with a normal six-year tenure cycle, the next few years will see one of two developments: a series of promotions to tenured positions will occur or a series of contract non-renewals will occur after tenure denials. Whichever occurs, junior faculty replacements will be needed whether or not individual programs expand or are reduced. The professional youthfulness of full-time faculty makes departments far from stable. Recommendations need to be made for developing quality during a time of relative flux.

In evaluating faculty quality, most previous studies used the degree qualifications for full professor as a primary criterion. Misner noted the historic emphasis on selecting for collegiate criminal justice programs faculty who had doctorates (1980, p. 157). Sherman (1978) noted that after the closing of Berkeley's School of Criminology, only nine doctoral programs in criminal justice or criminology existed in the country. In the future, then, the supply of doctoral level teachers in these fields will fall far short of the demand. Sherman's conclusion was telling: "It is unlikely that this group of

TABLE VII-1
DEMOGRAPHIC CHARACTERISTICS OF
FULL-TIME AND PART-TIME CRIMINAL JUSTICE FACULTY

		N	%
Age			
Less than 29 years		92	6.8
30 - 39 years		555	40.9
40 - 49 years		362	26.7
50 - 59 years		243	17.9
60 and above		92	6.7
Not reported		14	1.0
	Totals	1358	100.0
Sex			
Female		122	9.0
Male		1231	90.6
Not reported		5	0.4
	Totals	1358	100.0
Ethnicity			
Caucasian		1248	91.9
Black		44	3.2
Hispanic		13	1.0
Native American		29	2.1
Oriental		8	0.6
Asian		7	0.5
Other		2	0.1
Not reported		7	0.5
	Totals	1358	100.0

TABLE VII-2
DEMOGRAPHIC SAMPLE CHARACTERISTICS OF CRIMINAL
JUSTICE FACULTY BY FULL-TIME AND PART-TIME STATUS

	Full-Time		Part-Time	
	N	%	N	%
Age				
Less than 29 years	63	7.0	28	7.0
30 - 39 years	364	39.0	180	45.0
40 - 49 years	249	27.0	107	27.0
50 - 59 years	174	19.0	63	16.0
60 and above	70	8.0	18	5.0
Not reported	9	—	—	—
Totals	929	100.0	396	100.0
Sex				
Female	95	10.2	25	6.3
Male	834	89.8	371	93.7
Totals	929	100.0	396	100.0
Ethnicity				
Caucasian	860	92.6	360	90.9
Black	31	3.3	13	3.3
Hispanic	8	0.9	5	1.3
Native American	16	1.7	13	3.3
Oriental	5	0.5	3	0.8
Asian	7	0.8	—	—
Totals	929	100.0	396	100.0

faculty...will constitute more than 3 to 4 percent of the faculty in police education programs in the near future" (Sherman, 1978, p. 119).

TABLE VII-3
RANK, APPOINTMENT, AND TENURE CHARACTERISTICS OF
FULL-TIME CRIMINAL JUSTICE FACULTY

Academic Rank	N	%
Instructor/lecturer	161	17.3
Assistant professor	329	35.4
Associate professor	226	24.3
Full professor	167	18.0
Visiting professor	5	0.5
Adjunct	22	2.5
Other	19	2.0
Totals	929	100.0
Tenured		
Not tenured	463	49.4
Tenured	459	49.8
Not reported	7	—
Totals	929	100.0
Tenure Track Appointments	(N=461)	
On tenure track	342	74.2
Not on tenure track	119	25.8
Not reported	468	—
Totals	929	100.0
Years in Current Position	(N=904)	
Less than 5 years	446	49.0
5 - 9 years	287	32.0
10 - 14 years	122	13.5
15 or more years	49	5.5
Not reported	25	—
Totals	929	100.0

*Faculty Who Will Be Reviewed

Table VII-4 demonstrates that 33.1% of criminal justice faculty hold Ph.D.'s. Educators with professional degrees constitute a much lower percentage (3.9%) of faculty, and those with master's degrees comprise the largest single group of faculty in the Commission's study (36.7%). A breakdown of doctoral faculty by full and part time status indicates that full time teachers with doctorates outnumber part time teachers with doctorates by a ratio of more than four to one (45% as compared to 10%). What is less obvious is the proportion of educators with J.D.'s teaching full time to those teaching part time. Table VII-5 demonstrates that the percentage of teachers with J.D.'s in part-time appointments exceeds the percentage in full-time appointments by more than two to one (25% as compared to 11.3%). These data have two implications for faculty assessment: 1. Statistically part-time faculty are less well-trained in scholarship and should therefore not be doing any minor teaching of criminal justice at the academic level, and 2. Because an unusual relationship exists between criminal justice educators and lawyers, criminal justice faculties can use lawyers as specialists outside the academy to provide regular, part-time instruction.

TABLE VII-4
HIGHEST DEGREES HELD BY CRIMINOLOGY/CRIMINAL JUSTICE FACULTY

	N	%
Bachelor's	107	7.9
Master's	495	36.7
J.D./L.L.B.	188	13.9
Ph.D.	446	33.1
Professional degree (DPA, DSW, D. Crim.)	53	3.9
Other	17	1.3
Not reported	43	3.2
Total	1,349	100.0

An examination of 465 teachers by their fields of study is seen in Table VII-6. The large proportion of sociologists (40.2%) attests to the difficulty criminology and criminal justice have had establishing themselves as unique fields with distinct bodies of knowledge and methods. The low proportion of doctorates in criminology or criminal justice (11.7%, combined) probably implies as much about various needs in the

TABLE VII-5
FACULTY HOLDING DOCTORATES BY FULL-TIME AND PART-TIME STANDINGS

	Full-Time		Part-Time	
	N	%	N	%
Ph.D	415	45.0	40	10.1
J.D.	104	11.3	99	25.0
Other doctorate	50	5.3	2	00.5
Non-doctorate	359	38.6	255	64.5
Totals	929	100.0	396	100.0

market place for graduates with degrees as about the low number of graduates with degrees. The small proportion of J.D.'s or LL.B.'s in faculty positions (Table VII-4 shows 2.4%, combined) suggests that legal salaries are more lucrative than academic salaries; academe is probably not attractive to holders of these degrees except as a source of supplementary income.

TABLE VII-6
MAJOR FIELD OF STUDY FOR Ph.D. HOLDERS
(N=465)

Major Field	N	%
Sociology	187	40.2
Political Science	46	9.8
Psychology	44	9.4
Criminal justice	32	6.8
Criminology	23	4.9
Education	15	3.2
History	13	2.8
Public administration	12	2.5
Social science	10	2.1
Government	9	1.9
Other	74	15.3
Total	465	100.0

Relatively few criminal justice educators have entered the field directly after completing their graduate degrees. Table VII-7 indicates that although many criminal justice educators have had some teaching experience prior to their current positions, 35.6% have had none, including those who moved directly from an agency into teaching. Some criminal justice

TABLE VII-7
TEACHING EXPERIENCE PRIOR TO PRESENT POSITION
FOR FULL- AND PART-TIME FACULTY.

Experience	N	%
None	483	35.6
Taught in criminology/ criminal justice	704	51.8
Taught but not in criminology/ criminal justice	171	12.6
Totals	1,358	100.0

educators must have background and training that is entirely academic, and Table VII-8 does reveal a small group (8.4%) of them who were either graduate assistants at or otherwise associated with an educational institution before receiving their graduate degrees.

TABLE VII-8
WORK EXPERIENCE PATTERNS
PRIOR TO PURSUING HIGHEST DEGREE

Work Experience	N	%
Not reported	33	2.4
Worked full time		
Criminal justice agency	495	36.5
2-year institution	55	4.1
4-year or graduate institution	103	7.6
Non-criminal justice employment	156	11.5
Worked part time		
Criminal justice agency	22	1.6
2-year institution	5	0.4
4-year or graduate institution	23	1.7
Non-criminal justice employment	66	4.9
Graduate assistant	114	8.4
Not employed	139	10.2
Other	147	10.8
Totals	1358	100.0

The most common entry into criminal justice education is through experience in a law enforcement agency. The John Jay study revealed that over 70% of the surveyed faculty had experience in the criminal justice system (Berger; in Pearson, et al., 1980, p. 54). Sherman's report confirmed the high numbers of experienced agency personnel teaching in academic programs and documented the ensuing tensions between scholars and professionals. Sherman noted the "clear tendency of the colleges hiring the faculty to trade off degrees for practical experience in their criteria for selection" (Sherman, 1978, p. 121). Within faculties a tension sometimes exists between the "outsiders" or those solely from academe and the "insiders" or those with sworn police experience. The tension is not limited to criminal justice; it exists in all social science disciplines attempting to train professionals. Hoffman, Snell, and Webb state:

> In criminal justice education, the problem is the priority placed on the staffing of faculty with criminal justice backgrounds or the recruitment of individuals with master's and doctorates in the field. Once again, one can view with alarm the problems of both. One can imagine a Ph.D. in corrections who holds particular theories but in practice has never been within even a few blocks of a detention center or halfway house. On the other hand,

TABLE VII-9
TYPE OF CRIMINAL JUSTICE AGENCY EXPERIENCE

Type	N	%
Local law enforcement	263	47.0
State law enforcement	36	6.7
Local probation/parole	33	6.1
State institutional corrections	51	9.4
Local courts	21	3.0
Local institutional corrections	19	3.5
U.S. military	11	2.0
State probation/parole	10	1.8
Other	104	19.3
Totals	538	100.0

there are examples of those heavily oriented towards experience whose lectures never rise above the levels of a rehash of war stories (p.57).

The most glaring problem among experienced personnel may not be the breadth of their understanding but rather the narrowness of their vision. Tables VII-9 and VII-10 indicate that most experienced agency personnel come not from state or federal agencies but from local law enforcement. These statistics imply a potential provincialism among these faculty members who may emphasize local problems and issues rather than theory at state, national and international levels. A lack of diverse agency experience inevitably hinders those faculty members' ability to make policy and develop methodologies.

Because the statistics indicate a disproportionately large concentration of law enforcement personnel in criminal justice faculties, little seems to have changed since Sherman's study, and the pattern seems as rigid now as it did in 1965 (see W.P.

TABLE VII-10
TYPE OF CRIMINAL JUSTICE AGENCY EXPERIENCE BY
FULL-TIME AND PART-TIME

Type	Full-time N	Faculty %	Part-time N	Faculty %
Local law enforcement	143	46.0	106	49.5
State law enforcement	35	11.0	17	7.9
Local probation/parole	18	6.0	14	6.5
State institutional corrections	16	5.0	11	5.1
Local courts	10	3.0	11	5.1
Local institutional corrections	11	4.0	53	- -
Other	79	25.0	—	31.0
Totals	312	100.0	212	100.0

Brown, "Police and the Academic World," *Police Chief,* 1965, cited in Sherman, 1978, p. 125). Moreover, the different educational backgrounds of full-time and part-time faculty in agency experience seems clearer than ever. Whereas more full-time faculty have higher degrees, more part-time faculty have agency experience (34% of full-time; 54% of part-time). Part-time faculty, then, seem to be selected from a professional rather than from an academic milieu. Historically the commitment to teaching in a professional environment is probably slight, and the conceptual framework of any subject matter is generally not well articulated.

How individuals learned about their faculty jobs is a process which reflects poorly not only on educational institutions but also on professional organizations in criminology and criminal justice. In a study sponsored by the Commission, George Felkenes established how a group of criminal justice educators learned about and obtained their current positions. His results indicate that

> the most frequent means by which the respondents became aware of their present positions was through personal contacts in the field. Professional publications were the second most likely notification source (10.6%) (Felkenes, 1980, pp. 8-10)

Of Felkenes' group, 55.3% reported that they had learned of their present positions through "personal contacts" (Table VII-11). Felkenes' finding reinforces the impression made by earlier Commission data that the field is closed and parochial in that a network of personal contacts is more effective in announcing jobs and placing candidates than the professional organizations. Unlike such established groups as the Modern Language Association or the American Historical Association that hold annual conventions as organized recruitment forums, professional organizations representing criminal justice have failed to develop organized professional recruitment programs. Professional organizations like the A.S.C. and the A.C.J.S. must actively establish forums for employment. Individual institutions and departments should search for criminal justice educators through A.S.C. and A.C.J.S.

Individuals may enter the field of criminal justice education three ways: 1. those who are predominantly young, who proceed from college to graduate work with little agency experience and enter the field as academics, 2. those who having

TABLE VII-11
MEANS OF NOTIFICATION OF CURRENT POSITION

Means of Notification	Frequency	Percentage of Sample
Professional Publication	10	10.6
Recruiting Team	8	8.5
Personal Contacts	52	55.3
Associates	3	3.2
Recruiting Flyer	3	3.2
National Employment Listing Service	4	4.2
Promotion	3	3.2
Other	11	11.6
Total	94	100.0

Source: Felkenes, George T., *The Criminal Justice Doctorate: A Study of Doctoral Programs in the United States*, 1980, p. 11.

been attracted to teaching through agency or enforcement experience, seek new careers in the academy, and 3. those having professional degrees in law, education, or other fields and having had only part-time appointments in the academy who enter the field to provide supplementary educations. Career patterns range from academics to second careerists to peripheral adjunct personnel.

If criminal justice is to develop a base of knowledge, refine and extend its methodologies, formulate public policy, and substantiate its theories, it must have a committed faculty of trained scholars to do the necessary research. To achieve their goals, criminal justice departments, with the help of professional organizations, must actively seek doctorates committed to the academy rather than to the agency.

Chapter VIII

RESEARCH AND SCHOLARSHIP

One recurring finding in the Joint Commission's study is that research has not been developed in criminal justice. The Joint Commission has tried to examine the relationship between research and criminal justice education.

From one perspective, that relationship is part of a larger inquiry concerning criminal justice education and the knowledge cycle in criminal justice (For a useful collection of conceptual writings on the knowledge cycle, see Robert F. Rich, ed., *The Knowledge Cycle*, Sage, 1981). More specifically, what is and what should be the role of criminal justice education in the three basic elements of the knowledge cycle--the creation of knowledge, the diffusion of knowledge, and the utilization of knowledge?

Research may be considered the equivalent to the creation of knowledge. In a newly evolving field like criminal justice, forces within the field and those outside it have influenced attitudes toward research and have caused criminal justice educators to value research less than is desirable.

Criminal justice education developed in response to dramatic social changes that occurred in the 1960's. The following recommendation was made in 1973 by the National Advisory Commission on Criminal Justice Standards and Goals:

Criminal justice system curriculum and programs

should be established by agencies of higher education to unify the body of knowledge in law enforcement, criminology, social science, criminal law,
public administration, and corrections, and to serve
as a basis for preparing persons to work in the
criminal justice system (p. 78).

This recommendation codified federal policy on criminal
justice education and constituted a major external force shaping criminal justice education's attitude toward research. The
recommendation advocated establishing criminal justice
education programs to unify an existing body of knowledge
rather than advocating research to produce such knowledge.
Criminal justice education's objective, therefore, was not to
create new knowledge in the field but to unify and disseminate
existing knowledge to individuals working in the criminal
justice system.

Consequently, criminal justice education, influenced by an
external force of national policy, emphasized the dissemination
of knowledge rather than the creation of knowledge. The implementation of national policy crystallized an orientation
toward dissemination as seen in the history of the Law Enforcement Education Program (L.E.E.P.). A major source of
federal funding for criminal justice education, L.E.E.P. was
specifically designed to provide educational opportunities for
individuals employed in the criminal justice system as well as
for those who would be employed in it. L.E.E.P. guaranteed
that there would be future students in place to receive the
knowledge criminal justice education was to disseminate.

In response to national policy, criminal justice education
developed an internal apparatus and an ethos geared to
disseminating knowledge. The administration of criminal
justice education, its students, and especially its faculty
focussed upon teaching, an art of disseminating knowledge.

Criminal justice education can be a two-year, four-year, or
graduate field of study. Although graduate institutions are
considered to focus on research and the creation of knowledge,
two-year colleges are considered to focus on the dissemination
of knowledge. Approximately half of the criminal justice programs in this country are in two-year schools, signifying the
widespread acceptance of the dissemination of knowledge as
criminal justice's primary task.

Some of the data on the allocation and use of resources in
four-year criminal justice programs discussed in Chapter IV

reinforce the fact that administrators accept and maintain the dissemination of knowledge as criminal justice's function. These data indicate that most resources are committed to teaching, not to research. More than 25% of institutions responding indicated that they use five or more part-time faculty and almost 65% indicated that they use some part-time faculty. The extensive use of part-time faculty signifies an emphasis on teaching, not on research. More than 80% of the programs reported academic year teaching assignments of six or more courses, a relatively heavy commitment of resources to teaching.

Table VIII-1 provides data on faculty activity in teaching and research. More than 55% of full-time faculty reported

TABLE VIII-1
TIME SPENT ON ACADEMIC ACTIVITIES

	N	%
Teaching		
None	28	3.0
Less than 25%	106	11.4
25% - 49%	276	29.7
50% - 74%	365	39.3
75% or more	154	16.6
TOTALS	929	100.0
Research		
None	276	29.7
Less than 25%	527	56.7
25% - 49%	106	11.4
50% - 74%	18	1.9
75% or more	2	—
TOTALS	929	100.0

spending more than 50% of their time teaching. Approximately two percent of this group reported spending more than 50%
of their time on research. If criminal justice is to expand its
knowledge base and develop as a serious field of study, it must
recruit new faculty from research-oriented doctorates, and its
established faculty must redirect their efforts into research.

Table VIII-2 illustrates the well-known fact that the more
advanced the educational level of the students, the lighter the
teaching load will be for faculty. Professors teaching freshmen
and sophomores report teaching more courses per year than do

TABLE VIII-2
TEACHING LOADS OF FULL-TIME FACULTY

No. of Courses/Academic Year	N*	%
Freshman-Sophomore Level		
Less than 5 Courses	403	66.0
5 - 9 Courses	127	21.0
10 - 14 Courses	59	10.0
15 and more	20	3.0
TOTALS	609	100.0
Junior-Senior Level		
Less than 5 Courses	471	78.0
5 - 9 Courses	119	20.0
10 - 14 Courses	9	1.4
15 or more	4	0.6
Not reported	-	-
TOTALS	603	100.0
Graduate Level (M.A. and Ph.D.)		
Less than 5 Courses	340	96.0
5 - 9 Courses	13	3.5
10 or more	2	0.5
Not reported	-	-
TOTALS	355	100.0

*Total N for each level varies since data is reported for only those
faculty who are teaching at each level.

professors teaching juniors and seniors. All undergraduate instructors apparently teach more than graduate professors.
Although 66% of professors teaching freshmen and
sophomores reported teaching fewer than 5 courses per year,
78% of professors teaching junior and seniors reported a
similar load, and 96% of graduate professors indicated
teaching fewer than five courses per year. More striking is a
comparison between undergraduate and graduate workloads
of professors teaching five to nine courses per year. Although
the same percentage of undergraduate teachers reported
teaching five to nine courses (21% of the lower division; 20% of
the upper division), only 3.5% of graduate professors reported
teaching five to nine courses annually.

The sizes of undergraduate and graduate criminal justice
classes also indicated greater faculty workloads at
undergraduate levels. At the freshman-sophomore level, more
than 60% of the faculty reported classes of thirty or more
students; at the junior-senior level, 53% of the faculty reported
classes of thirty or more students. However, at the graduate
level, only 5.4% of the professoriate reported classes of thirty
or more students. These percentages indicate that
undergraduate teachers' workloads reduce their potential time
for research. Graduate faculty have fewer classes with fewer
students and therefore should have more time to devote to
research (see Table VIII-3). Although this data represent time
allocations common to all academic disciplines at most universities, they have a unique meaning for criminal justice, because
they indicate a lack of research vital to the field's growth.

If a field of study is to create and not just disseminate
knowledge, its faculty must be trained to do research or create
knowledge. The following findings are from the Commission's
study of faculty.

1. Approximately 14% of all criminal justice faculty
    possess the traditional research degree, a doctorate.

2. Only 45% of all full-time criminal justice faculty
    possess a doctorate.

The proportion of faculty who are traditionally trained to
create knowledge is strikingly small when all faculty are considered and still small when only full-time faculty are considered. The data indicate that faculty in the field place
relatively little emphasis on research or, presumably, on
publication of that research.

TABLE VIII-3
CURRENT ACADEMIC ASSIGNMENT

Average Class Size		N	%
Freshman-Sophomore Level			
Less than 19		66	11.0
20 - 29		165	27.2
30 - 39		190	31.4
40 - 99		140	23.1
100 - 199		28	4.7
200 - 299		8	1.3
300 and above		8	1.3
	TOTALS	605	100.0
Junior-Senior Level			
Less than 19		102	17.1
20 - 29		178	29.8
30 - 39		153	25.7
40 - 99		140	23.4
100 - 199		19	3.2
200 - 299		3	0.5
300 and above		2	0.3
	TOTALS	597	100.0
Graduate Level			
Less than 9		86	24.2
10 - 19		185	52.1
20 - 29		65	18.3
30 and above		19	5.4
	TOTALS	355	100.0

Deciding how much time to spend on research may be affected by constraining teaching loads or administrative policies. The number of articles published may result from the time available to write. The emphasis placed on research is probably more a matter of institutional policy and administrative decision-making than faculty preference; however, the following data in Table VIII-4 indicate that faculty have different views of research.

1. Approximately 87% of the total faculty sample reported spending 24% or less of their time on research. When asked what percentage of time they would like to spend on research, 77% of the faculty responded they would prefer spending 24% or less of their time.

2. Approximately 95% of the faculty reported spending 24% or less of their time writing. When asked what percentage of time they would like to spend writing, 90% responded they would prefer spending 24% or less of their time.

The data indicate that faculty prefer a status quo with teaching taking precedence over research in criminal justice education. The time faculty spend on academic activities indicates the relative emphasis they place on teaching:

1. Almost 30% of full-time faculty report they spend no time on research. Only 3% of faculty report spending no time on teaching.

2. Almost 60% of full-time faculty report spending 35% or less of their time on research. Approximately 14% of the faculty report spending 25% or less of their time on research.

These findings and some of the findings on publication reported in Chapter VII underscore the relatively low commitment of criminal justice faculty to research. The data in Table VIII-5 further demonstrate criminal justice faculty experiences with publishing. Most faculty are willing to commit only a small amount of time to research writing, and publication but commit a great amount of time to teaching.

The Joint Commission also solicited faculty self-assessments to learn how the professoriate react to their

TABLE VIII-4

CURRENT AND DESIRED TIME ALLOCATIONS FOR FACULTY ACTIVITIES

N=1354

Activity	% of current time spent (% responding)				% of time desired (% responding)			
	0-24	27-49	50-74	75 plus	0-24	25-49	50-74	75 plus
Teaching	22.0%	23.5%	22.1%	30.5%	25.6%	30.5%	13.4%	23.4%
Research	87.4%	2.4%	------	10.2%	77.3%	3.9%	.7%	18.1%
Writing	95.5%	3.5%	------	4.0%	90.1%	1.5%	------	8.5%
Counseling/Advising Students Formally Assigned	97.0%	1.5%	1.5%	------	97.3%	1.6%	1.1%	------
Providing Public Service to Criminal Justice Agencies	96.5%	1.4%	0.8%	1.2%	96.5%	2.9%	0.1%	0.5%
Departmental/University Administration	88.2%	4.1%	1.6%	6.1%	93.0%	2.4%	0.7%	3.9%

TABLE VIII-5
PERCENTAGE OF FULL-TIME FACULTY NOT HAVING
PUBLISHED FOR SIX MAJOR PUBLICATION CATEGORIES
n=909

Publication Category	% of Faculty Who Have Not Published
Books	77.6
Edited Books	84.5
Monographs	75.5
Chapters in Books	69.9
Government Reports	69.9
Refereed Journal Articles	52.3
Non-Refereed Journal Articles	66.7

workloads and how they evaluate their work in the field. Table VIII-6 summarizes the self-assessments in several traditional faculty activities. Remembering the relative commitments to teaching and research, compare the degrees of importance faculty members assigned to each activity. "Teaching undergraduate courses" was given a rating of 4 or 5 (5 = great importance) by more than 82% of the faculty. "Assisting students in their professional development" was also rated highly; more than 88% gave it a rating of at least 4. By contrast, "theory testing and development" was rated at least 4 by less than half the faculty (46.9%). "Methodology developments" received a 44% response of 4 or 5, and approximately half of the faculty (51.6%) rated the writing of research articles highly. Faculty self-assessments reinforce the statistical information about the state of the criminal justice field.

The problems of a faculty oriented towards teaching, however, go beyond their neglect of research. Charles Saunders realized that as the number of criminal justice students increased disproportionately to the number of criminal justice faculty, the quality of teaching would decline (Saunders, 1970, cited in Sherman, 1978, p. 131). If a "typical" undergraduate teacher with thirty students per course is teaching from five to nine courses a year, the sheer volume of student work the teacher must evaluate becomes overwhelming. Those teachers cannot dream of doing research; their course loads alone prevent it. Faculty-student ratios must be reduced not only to allow faculty time for research, but also to insure the quality of instruction. With time allocated fairly between teaching and scholarship, the faculty could better serve themselves, their students, and their field.

Perhaps more than any other criterion, publication has become a touchstone for assessing faculty quality and "professionalism." Two recent Joint Commission sponsored studies (Regoli and Miracle, 1980; DeZee, 1980) used both publication statistics and faculty assessments of their own publications to determine the quality of programs, the productivity of the professoriate, and their professionalism. DeZee cautioned:

> The use of a publication index is, of course, subject to some important limitations. The lower scores of some institutions may reflect current priorities and orientations. That is, the 'publish or perish' syndrome may or may not exist at some institutions,

TABLE VIII-6
PERSONAL IMPORTANCE ASSIGNED TO FACULTY WORKLOAD ACTIVITIES AND TO FACULTY ROLE

Activity	Not reported	No Importance 1 n (%)	2 n (%)	3 n (%)	4 n (%)	Great Importance 5 n (%)	Total n (%)
Conference Participation A.C.J.S. and Regions	45	116 (13.1)	125 (14.1)	240 (27.1)	223 (25.2)	180 (20.4)	884 (100.0)
Conference Participation A.S.C.	64	139 (16.1)	125 (14.5)	260 (30.1)	195 (22.5)	146 (16.9)	865 (100.0)
Conference Participation Other,	43	43 (4.9)	109 (12.3)	277 (31.3)	263 (29.7)	194 (21.9)	886 (100.0)
Departmental Administrative Tasks	29	103 (11.4)	169 (18.8)	303 (33.7)	206 (22.9)	119 (13.2)	900 (100.0)
Providing Technical Assistance to Criminal Justice Agencies	32	84 (9.4)	116 (12.9)	218 (24.3)	248 (27.6)	231 (25.8)	897 (100.0)
Consulting (private)	49	128 (14.5)	151 (17.2)	278 (31.6)	192 (21.8)	131 (14.9)	880 (100.0)
Curriculum Development	24	20 (2.2)	33 (3.6)	157 (17.3)	301 (33.3)	394 (43.5)	905 (100.0)

Teaching Undergraduate Courses	24	16 (1.8)	33 (3.6)	112 (12.4)	219 (24.2)	525 (58.0)	905 (100.0)
Teaching Graduate Courses	96	185 (22.2)	32 (3.8)	138 (15.4)	237 (28.5)	251 (30.1)	833 (100.0)
Theory Testing and Development	54	87 (9.9)	117 (13.4)	261 (29.8)	249 (28.5)	161 (18.4)	875 (100.0)
Providing Agency Training	32	149 (16.6)	139 (15.5)	223 (24.9)	200 (22.3)	186 (20.7)	897 (100.0)
Evaluating Local Agency Projects	43	154 (17.4)	126 (14.2)	255 (28.8)	243 (27.4)	108 (12.2)	886 (100.0)
Methodology Developments	49	97 (11.0)	115 (13.1)	281 (31.9)	246 (28.0)	141 (16.0)	880 (100.0)
Writing Grants	32	114 (12.7)	129 (14.4)	291 (32.4)	218 (24.3)	145 (16.2)	897 (100.0)
Assisting Students in Their Professional Development	19	6 (0.7)	20 (2.2)	81 (8.9)	285 (31.8)	518 (56.9)	910 (100.0)
Writing Research Articles for Journals	28	71 (7.9)	116 (12.9)	249 (27.6)	234 (26.0)	231 (25.6)	901 (100.0)
Writing Other Journal Articles	32	86 (9.6)	130 (14.5)	269 (30.0)	240 (26.8)	172 (19.2)	897 (100.0)
Writing Textbooks for the Student Audience	33	131 (14.6)	178 (19.9)	261 (29.1)	209 (23.3)	117 (13.1)	896 (100.0)
Writing Books for the Professional Audience	34	126 (14.1)	131 (14.6)	238 (26.6)	231 (25.8)	169 (18.9)	895 (100.0)

TABLE VIII-7
SELF REPORTED PUBLICATIONS
ACTIVITY OF FULL-TIME FACULTY

Type	N	%
Number of Books		
None	721	77.6
1	106	11.4
2	53	5.7
3	14	1.5
4	7	0.1
5 or more	28	3.0
TOTALS	929	100.0
Number of Edited Books		
None	785	84.5
1	78	8.4
2	30	3.2
3	11	1.2
4	9	1.0
5 or more	16	1.7
TOTALS	929	100.0
Number of Monographs		
None	701	75.5
1	94	10.1
2	54	5.8
3	31	3.3
4	13	1.4
5 or more	36	3.9
TOTALS	929	100.0
Number of Chapters in Book		
None	649	69.9
1	107	11.5
2	66	7.2
3	37	3.9
4	27	2.9
5 or more	43	4.6
TOTALS	929	100.0

TABLE VIII-7 cont.
SELF REPORTED PUBLICATIONS
ACTIVITY OF FULL-TIME FACULTY

Type	N	%
Number of Government Reports		
None	650	69.9
1	77	8.4
2	58	6.2
3	37	3.9
4	23	2.5
5 or more	84	9.1
TOTALS	929	100.0
Number of Articles in Refereed Journals		
None	486	52.3
1 - 2	150	16.1
3 - 4	93	10.0
5 - 10	104	11.2
11 - 15	34	4.0
16 - 20	24	2.6
21 - 30	14	1.5
31 - 40	13	1.4
41 - 50	2	0.1
50 or more	9	1.0
TOTALS	929	100.0
Number of Articles in Non-Refereed Journals		
None	620	66.7
1 - 2	118	12.7
3 - 4	72	7.8
5 - 10	50	5.4
11 - 15	21	2.3
16 - 20	14	1.5
21 - 30	13	1.4
31 - 40	10	1.0
41 - 50	3	0.1
50 or more	8	0.1
TOTALS	929	100.0

while others may place greater emphasis on books
and monograph publications . . . (DeZee, 1980, p.
21).

The Joint Commission's data on publication appear in Table
VIII-7. With the exception of publishing in refereed journals,
in which 52.3% of the faculty reported publishing, between
67% and 86% report not having published in each of the
categories considered. Of those who have published at all, approximately 10% appear to have published in only one of each
type of publication. Examples of frequent publication are proportionately rare regardless of the type of publication. The
data, therefore, suggest a certain complacency about
publishing, as if producing one article fulfilled a requirement
and as if to publish widely was to deviate from rather than con-
form to the field's professional standards.

The Joint Commission's data on publication both comple-
ment and contrast with the data assembled by Regoli and
Miracle in their study of professionalism. They attempted to
demonstrate a correlation between journal prestige, as perceived by A.S.C. and A.C.J.S. members, and the "professionalism"
of the respondents. Their data are confusing, and they conclude by calling for more work "focusing on the effect (if any)
professionalism has . . . on journal productivity . . . " (p. 30).
However, the apparently confusing and "substantively meaningless" (p. 30) data are valuable, because they indicate, in a
perverse way, that journal publication and a history of publications do not greatly influence the profession's self-perceptions.
The Joint Commission's data indicate that among full-time
faculty publications are not as compelling a personal priority
as they should be, or there would be more of them. The Commission must recommend, therefore, that criminal justice
educators publish more research, not for the sake of volume only but for depth, not to amass a good history for tenure or promotion but to amass a body of knowledge for the field. To
disseminate knowledge to all members of the field, large quan-
tities of quality publications are essential. Perhaps publications can provide the sense of unity to the field that the national professional organizations have failed to achieve. By
establishing a canon of texts for its teachers and by initiating
dialogues among scholars widely separated by distance and
point of view, widespread publishing might remedy the
parochialism of the faculty and reinforce to other university

departments the academic legitimacy of criminal justice and criminology.

Table VIII-8 provides salary ranges for a contractual year reported by full-time faculty. Most full-time faculty (57.8%) report a salary between $14,000 and $21,999, with the highest proportion in the $16,000-$17,999 range. In light of the publication data, the salary statistics confirm the Commission's earlier findings that criminal justice faculty are young, still at junior rank, and hold relatively low-paying positions.

What is revealing, however, is the sharp difference between full-time and part-time compensation. Part-time faculty are paid for each course they teach, and the Joint Commission

TABLE VIII-8
SALARY RANGES OF FULL-TIME FACULTY

Salary	n	%
Below $10,000	4	0.4
$10,000 - $11,999	8	0.9
$12,000 - $13,999	41	4.5
$14,000 - $15,999	104	11.4
$16,000 - $17,999	162	17.8
$18,000 - $19,000	133	14.6
$20,000 - $21,999	126	13.8
$22,000 - $23,999	79	8.7
$24,000 - $25,999	68	7.5
$26,000 - $27,999	57	6.3
$28,000 - $29,999	38	4.2
$30,000 - $31,999	30	3.3
$32,000 - $33,999	23	2.5
$34,000 - $35,999	8	0.9
$36,000 - $37,999	7	0.8
$38,000 - $39,999	3	0.3
$40,000 - $41,999	8	0.9
$42,000 - $43,999	2	0.2
$44,000 - $45,999	5	0.5
$46,000 - $47,999	5	0.5
$50,000 and above	1	0.1
Not Reported	17	--
TOTAL	929	100.0

found a very low per-course pay scale. As Table VIII-9 indicates, 64% of the 355 part-time respondents reported that they were paid less than a thousand dollars per course. Part-time instructors, of course, can never approach the financial compensation paid to their full-time colleagues for course work. As a source of inexpensive labor, part-time faculty not only cannot give the same kind of commitment to their students and their field as full-time faculty, but because they are often hired on a per term basis, they cannot bring continuity to their own work or to the institution's program of study. (See Sherman, 1978, p. 95). Although the use of part-time faculty may reduce the teaching loads of full-time faculty and hence free them for research, the exploitation of part-time faculty is an embarrassment to the academic community. The part-time faculty's commitments are minimal, because the commitments made to them are minimal. Moreover, the use of a large part-time faculty hurts an individual criminal justice program and hinders the national growth of the field. The institution, the field, and the students benefit only when the use of part-time faculty is carefully limited.

Given the status of part-time faculty in criminal justice programs, the Commission concurs with the recommendations of Sherman (1978), which were developed from recommendations in the A.C.J.S. Accreditation-Standards in 1976. The use of part-time instructors in criminal justice education must be minimized, and part-time faculty should never be an integral part of any program at any level. Although it is difficult to prescribe precise ratios of full-time to part-time faculty, the Commission agrees that no more than one-third of a student's course work should be taught by part-time faculty, and that no more than one fourth of a faculty's total workload should be delegated to part-time faculty.

TABLE VIII-9
AMOUNT PAID PER COURSE TO PART-TIME FACULTY

	N	%
Below $600	42	11.8
$600 - $999	184	51.8
$1,000 - $1,499	80	22.5
$1,500 - $1,999	22	6.2
$2,000 or more	14	3.9
Not paid on per course basis	13	3.7
TOTAL	355	100.0

FACULTY CHARACTERISTICS

Of major concern within the criminal justice field has been the difference between two-year, junior college programs and four-year, university and graduate level programs. Community colleges account for a large portion of crime-related programs (Bennett and Marshall, 1979), and because these programs tend to center on task proficiency (Brandstatter and Hoover, 1976; Sherman et al. 1978) and vocational issues (Tenny, 1971; Adams 1976; Sherman 1978), some critics have argued that criminal justice education lacks academic credibility. In contrast, four-year college and university programs follow professional, social science and liberal arts models (Tenney, 1971; Senna, 1974; Kuykendall, 1977) and have developed a body of knowledge about crime and society's reaction to criminal behavior (see Morn, 1980).

The quality of teaching is similarly divided according to institutional level. Community colleges hire faculty with practical experience while universities stress academic credentials (Hoffman, Snell, Webb, 1976). Moreover, the tendency of community colleges to attract agency-experienced personnel perpetuates a field that does limited research (Sherman, 1978). In addition to institutional differences, the individual professional orientation of faculty members separates faculty into teachers or researchers. Conrad and Myren suggest that faculty perceive a difference between "criminal justice educators" and "criminologists." The former traditionally think of themselves as practitioners; the latter, as academic sociologists (Conrad and Myren, 1979, pp. 26-27; 10-11; see also Morn, 1980, p. 26). Other Joint Commission supported studies, like that of Regoli and Miracle, attempted to measure the "professionalism" of criminal justice educators and criminologists according to the professional organizations to which respondents belonged (Regoli and Miracle, 1980, p. 11).

The Joint Commission study critically examined the interactions of education, experience and self-perceptions in determining faculty attitudes toward teaching and research. The study asked faculty to rate themselves in a number of areas, including quality of teaching and research, type of research (applied or basic), level of research, whether their research was policy oriented and was contributing to the development of the field (see Table VIII-10). Faculty were also asked if they considered themselves scholars, educators, intellectuals, professionals, or even blue collar workers, and they were asked their

TABLE VIII-10
SELF-ASSESSMENT AND CRIMINAL JUSTICE AGENCY
EXPERIENCE OF FACULTY PRIOR TO FULL-TIME
ACADEMIC EMPLOYMENT

	(N=616) No Full-Time Criminal Justice Experience	(N=278) Full-Time Criminal Justice Experience	x^2	Gamma
Quality of teaching	8.15	8.37	4.08	.12
Quality of research	6.37	5.54	24.17**	-.28
Type of research	5.20	4.59	17.69**	-.19
Extent of research involvement	5.06	4.10	21.15**	-.25
Extent of policy orientation	4.80	4.33	9.81*	-.17
Level of contribution to theory	4.63	3.68	27.42**	-.29
Extent a scholar	6.83	5.97	34.33**	-.32
Extent an educator	8.13	8.34	1.31	.04
Extent an intellectual	7.24	6.33	38.38**	-.37
Extent a professional	8.38	8.77	8.05*	.15
Extent a blue collar worker	2.30	2.96	20.15**	.28
Too much emphasis on empirical research	4.67	4.30	8.40*	-.17
Rather work in C.J. agency	5.64	4.83	39.64	.39
Research should focus on agency problems	4.49	3.47	56.62	-.45
What is taught is too prescriptive	3.78	4.00	1.49	.08

* p less than .05
** p less than .01

beliefs about current research emphases and the apparent prescriptiveness of criminal justice education.

In Table VIII-11 faculty self-assessments are given according to type of educational institution. As may have been expected, two-year college teachers valued teaching and paraprofessionalism more highly than university teachers did. Individuals at higher level institutions were less positive about the quality of their teaching and less likely to view themselves either as educators or professionals. The university faculty certainly considered themselves teachers, but the two-year college faculty rated themselves more often as teachers first and foremost than did university faculty.

Table VIII-11 indicates that faculty in two year programs agreed more strongly than did university faculty that research was excessively emphasized, that they would rather work in a criminal justice agency, and that research should focus on agency problems. Moreover, two-year program respondents expressed less agreement that course content is too prescriptive than did those at four-year or university levels. When respondents were affiliated with higher level institutions, they objected less to empirical research, to a desire to work in an agency, and to lowering their commitment to solve agency problems. Those affiliated with higher level institutions more often thought that the field was excessively prescriptive.

Perceptions of the nature, quantity, and quality of research were also affected by institutional level. As Table VIII-11 indicates, the higher the level of the institution, the greater the belief in research and its quality. Moreover, four-year institutions were thought to be more closely associated with public policy formation than were community colleges. Not surprisingly, educators at the four-year university level believed that their research directly affected formulation and implementation of public policy.

In addition to institutional differences, the involvement with agencies by faculty affected self-assessments as seen in Table VIII-10. Although the differences between faculty with fulltime agency experience and those without it are less acute than the differences between two-year and four-year faculty, faculty without agency experience value research, theory-building and scholarship. Faculty with agency experience displayed great interest in empirical research and rated themselves comparatively higher in teaching quality and educational purpose.

Other dichotomies emerge from the data in Tables VIII-12

TABLE VIII-11
SELF-ASSESSMENT BY LEVEL OF INSTITUTIONAL
EMPLOYMENT

	Two-Year Program b (N=216)	Four-Year College (N=171)	(N=501)	University c/ x^2	Gamma
Quality of teaching	8.64	8.50	8.28	14.18*	-.18
Quality of research	5.84	6.11	6.68	26.48**	.22
Type of research	5.13	5.24	5.46	8.11	.10
Extent of research involvement	3.77	4.42	5.52	85.45**	.40
Extent of policy orientation	3.68	4.70	5.43	68.66**	.36
Level of contribution to theory	3.53	4.35	4.95	48.63**	.30
Extent a scholar	6.06	6.58	7.10	43.66**	.30
Extent an educator	8.69	8.53	8.23	16.20**	-.16
Extent an intellectual	6.69	7.22	7.39	23.27**	.20
Extent a professional	9.10	8.77	8.46	20.92	-.24
Extent a blue collar worker	3.18	2.30	2.38	19.83**	-.19
Too much emphasis on empirical research	3.54	3.43	3.19	8.40	-.13
Rather work in C.J. agency	3.11	2.38	2.18	37.07**	-.30
Research should focus on agency problems	4.43	3.66	3.35	48.54**	-.31
What taught is too prescriptive	3.62	4.01	4.14	15.93**	.18

a/Range on quality of teaching and quality of research = 1-poor, 10-excellent; range on type of research = 1-applied, 10-basic. Range on extent of research involvement through extent a blue collar worker = range on too much empirical research through research should focus on agency problems = 1- strongly disagree, 7 - strongly agree.

b/Mean score derived from unrecorded values of department variables.

c/Chi-square distribution derived from recorded values of dependent variables; quality of teaching to extent blue collar, 1, 2 = low; 3, 4, 5 = moderately low; 6, 7, 8, = moderately high; 9, 10 = high; too much emphasis on empirical research through research should focus on agency problems; 1, 2 = disagree; 3, 4, 5, = intermediate, 6, 7 = agree.

* p less than .05
** p less than .01

TABLE VIII-12
SELF-ASSESSMENT BY HIGHEST DEGREE AWARDED BY
DEPARTMENTAL UNIT

Item	$\bar{x}$ (N=214) Associate	$\bar{x}$ (N=209) Bachelor	$\bar{x}$ (N=336) Masters	$\bar{x}$ (N=145) Doctorate	x^2	Gamma
Quality of teaching	8.66	8.41	8.43	7.98	27.33**	-.19
Quality of research	5.82	6.00	6.63	7.14	48.91**	.26
Type of research	5.11	5.24	5.28	5.85	15.82	.11
Extent of research involvement	3.76	4.41	5.23	6.41	114.40**	.40
Extent of policy orientation	3.71	4.85	5.37	5.47	67.77**	.28
Level of contribution to theory	3.50	4.31	4.71	5.64	68.34**	.31
Extent a scholar	6.06	6.52	6.98	7.58	50.81**	.28
Extent an educator	8.71	8.57	8.38	7.78	16.20**	-.16
Extent an intellectual	6.70	7.12	7.36	7.64	27.99**	.20
Extent a professional	9.12	8.74	8.62	8.09	38.89**	-.25
Extent a blue collar worker	3.24	2.31	2.33	2.42	26.57**	-.17
Too much emphasis on empirical research	3.58	3.37	3.25	2.99	11.83	-.12
Rather work in C.J. agency	3.00	2.43	2.31	1.87	37.09**	-.27
Research should focus on agency problems	4.48	3.53	3.58	2.96	73.24**	-.29
What taught is too prescriptive	3.63	3.99	4.09	4.29	25.68**	.18

* p less than .05
** p less than .01

and VIII-13. The higher their degree, the greater was the commitment by faculty to research and theory over teaching, with those possessing a doctorate valuing research and theory most highly. Respondents without doctorates preferred applied research over theoretical research and regarded agency employment more favorably than did their university colleagues.

From these data emerge some very clear perceptions of faculty self-assessment, and these perceptions helped the Joint Commission in formulating its recommendations. There is a broad difference between scholarship, research and theory-building with faculty at advanced institutions who hold higher degrees and have scholarly backgrounds, and teaching, professionalism and administration with those in lower division programs, having limited professional degrees and agency or administrative backgrounds. The Joint Commission believes that faculty should be individuals with strong academic backgrounds, a commitment to research, and demonstrable teaching ability. Prior criminal justice or agency experience should not be a consideration in faculty hiring. Once someone has decided to enter the academic side of criminal justice, that individual must bring to it a personal sense of new commitment. This sense will differ from that of a career agency employee; it will be closer to that of the professional academic, regardless of field of interest.

Experience is important and will usually broaden an educator's perspective. Nevertheless, the Commission strongly believes that a good criminal justice educator, scholar or researcher, regardless of background, must demonstrate an aptitude for teaching and research and professional involvement. Moreover, they should assess their activities through participation in regional or national organizations and through research and publications.

It is clear that criminal justice and criminology are different from most academic fields in that they prepare practitioners to deal directly with minorities who are both victims of and suspects in crimes. Criminal justice education will benefit from faculty and staff whose ethnic composition corresponds to that of individuals involved with crime. The Commission believes strongly that minorities and women should be encouraged to pursue careers in criminal justice education. Hiring qualified women and minority faculty, and admitting qualified women and minority students will help the profession accurately reflect its subject matter.

Faculty quality may be assessed, but improving it is another

TABLE VIII-13
SELF-ASSESSMENT BY HIGHEST DEGREE HELD BY RESPONDENT

	x (N=430) Less than Ph.D. or Professional Doctorate	x (N=454) Ph.D. or Professional Doctorate	Item x^2	Gamma
Quality of teaching	8.56	8.26	9.38*	-.20
Quality of research	5.70	6.98	72.65**	.45
Type of research	4.98	5.62	21.91**	.22
Extent of research involvement	3.97	5.72	98.49**	.51
Extent of policy orientation	4.33	5.37	37.18**	.31
Level of contribution to theory	3.61	5.32	87.84**	.47
Extent a scholar	6.13	7.36	66.69**	.44
Extent an educator	8.66	8.18	21.88**	-.24
Extent an intellectual	6.78	7.61	36.99**	.34
Extent a professional	8.97	8.43	24.20**	-.26
Extent a blue collar worker	2.73	2.35	10.77**	-.16
Too much emphasis on empirical research	3.69	2.97	33.77**	-.30
Rather work in CJ agency	2.89	2.00	53.84	-.45
Research should focus on agency problems	4.23	3.16	65.68	-.45
What is taught is too prescriptive	3.70	4.28	19.11**	.25

* p less than .05   ** p less than .01

matter. Because criminal justice faculty are young both in age and in experience, great possibilities exist for improvement in the early stages of faculty members' careers.

The idea of "faculty development" grew in response to the student-initiated evaluations of the late 1960's and early 1970's, and was expanded due to a nationwide concern for a "humane" higher education environment (see Blackburn, et al., "Instructional Improvement Programs," in *Current Issues in Higher Education,* 1980, no. 1, pp. 32-48).

What students expect of their educational experiences may be instrumental in shaping emphases in a field of study. Curriculum issues and student influence in determining curricula were discussed in Chapter V. However, ways in which students in criminal justice may influence whether emphasis will be on research or teaching warrant some consideration.

Almost 75% of the criminal justice students surveyed by the Commission reported that they enrolled in criminal justice courses to prepare for a career or to take courses that were job-related. Approximately 62% agreed or strongly agreed that criminal justice education should emphasize job-related skills. These data indicate that the criminal justice student wants an education that will lead to a job and that will provide practical skills. These student expectations are not compatible with an emphasis on research which entails substantial uncertainty, abstraction and generality. These student expectations are also not conducive to a faculty with a strong commitment for research. Rather, they are likely to result in programs and faculty emphasizing the *dissemination* of practical knowledge, thus reinforcing the dominance of teaching in criminal justice education.

The Joint Commission views faculty development not as an exercise to placate students or as therapeutic introspection for individual faculty members but rather as a process essential to the growth of the field. To expand the base of knowledge and to graduate well-trained, motivated students who will become the future professionals in the field, a faculty must combine commitment to teaching with dedication to research. Young faculty have opportunities to develop as teachers and researchers. The impetus for their development should come not only from their institution or department but from the national organizations as well.

Relatively low allocations for faculty development (80% reported $294 or less per full-time employee) is another indication of emphasis on teaching rather than research. Support for non-teaching or research activities might be reimbursement to faculty for travel expenses to scholarly meetings. National and regional organizations should inform faculty of recent advances in theory and method and provide them with a forum for the exchange and criticism of ideas. The large proportion of recently appointed tenure-track faculty will make the next five years a critical period for faculty development and professional redirection.

The Commission is concerned not only with the quality of faculty, but with how they are utilized at various institutions. As the data reveal, criminal justice is a teacher's field, and a strong desire to teach can only help students. However, an unwillingness to do research can only hurt the field. Although large classes and heavy teaching loads may increase the number of criminal justice majors and graduates, these numbers can only detract from the effective good teaching of individual students. To best utilize a faculty, an institution should encourage and support research, as well as attempt to lower student-faculty ratios, especially in two and four year programs.

The rapid development of criminal justice education has institutionalized its strong orientation to only one element in the knowledge cycle. In the 1960's criminal justice hurriedly established structures for disseminating knowledge that have been the dominant orientation of criminal justice education. As the field developed, external and internal forces both determined and maintain dissemination of knowledge.

Criminal justice education's paramount need is to expand its emphasis on research. In its next stage of development, criminal justice education must emphasize building its capacity to do research and develop a research faculty capable of instilling in students a sense of basic inquiry.

Chapter IX

STUDENTS

Frequently criminal justice students have been perceived as "different" from their peers in other college majors. Their "difference" has not been seen as uniqueness but as a weakness characteristic of the major. Their purported defects included a limited academic ability and orientation, inappropriate motives like careers and income for attending college and an inability and unwillingness to participate in extracurricular activities. The view of criminal justice students as "different" originated during the 1960's when the typical criminal justice student was an inservice police officer, 25 to 40 years of age and the head of a family. Criminal justice students were indeed different in terms of the expectations of other students and faculty. The non-criminal justice student who took a criminal justice course as an elective was not prepared to discover that many, if not most, of the other students in the course were "cops." Traditional faculty members were probably equally surprised to discover police officers teaching criminal justice courses. To most students and faculty, criminal justice students and faculty *were* different.

Although the perceived differences were real, some perceived defects of criminal justice majors were also real. Early inservice criminal justice students were probably not very well prepared to become college students. Their study skills and writing skills were probably not what they should have been.

Moreover, criminal justice faculty probably held very low expectations for the academic performance of inservice students.

Many faculty members were not very well prepared to provide a rigorous education and to demand maximum performance from their students. Teachers who were ex-practitioners tended to over-identify with the plight of inservice students, and some were lenient with assignments and grades.

The lack of a developing body of knowledge on crime and criminal justice affected the perceptions of majors. It was reflected in the low conceptual level of criminal justice texts and teaching materials and made it difficult for the best of faculty and impossible for the worst to maintain adequate performance standards for students.

The institutional setting in which criminal justice developed also contributed to a negative image of criminal justice students. Criminal justice education did not usually develop at the premier institutions of higher education but tended to be established at commuter campuses and community colleges. The commuter campus emerged from the educational reform and curriculum experimentation of the 1960's and 70's. It is usually publicly funded, and students pay relatively low tuition. Consequently, a disproportionate number of minority, low income, and part-time students are found on commuter campuses. Additionally, many strong traditions of collegiate life associated with residential campuses do not exist on the commuter campus. When federal funding programs were widespread, Jencks and Riesman (1968, pp. 491-2) welcomed the community colleges and commuter schools as refreshing departures from traditional college and graduate education (see also Rudolph, 1977, p. 285). In light of the civil rights movement, these campuses provided educational opportunities for many students. Given the liberal temperament of the times, development of these campuses also coincided with the Safe Streets Act, the war on crime, and the development of the L.E.E.P. program.

Recent research has focused on the different kinds of effects commuting and residency may have on undergraduates. Chickering has argued that institutional differences only reinforce sociological ones: that poor, disadvantaged students commute and that the wealthy, privileged students live on campus (Chickering, 1974, pp. 40-41). In an unpublished study sponsored by the Joint Commission, C. Allen Pierce (1980) compared and contrasted commuting and residential students according to socio-economic values. Pierce viewed the differences as focusing on emotional impact and sociological effect. Residential students would interact actively with true peers in age and achievement and would use the campus as a base for all social and intellectual activities. Commuting students would be less committed to the institution, would see fewer "peers" in and outside the classroom, and would perceive the campus as an alien environment, not to be used but only to be visited. Moreover, Pierce noted that a proportionately higher number of residential students had college-educated parents, whereas most commuter students would probably be first-generation undergraduates in their families (see Pierce, 1981, p. 48-50).

The early evolution of criminal justice involved inservice students, inadequate faculty, an inadequate base of knowledge, and the growth of commuter schools and community colleges. It was understandable that criminal justice students were perceived as less qualified and less able than others. Unfortunately, certain memories are long lasting to the present time. The Joint Commission, in examining criminal justice students, was guided by an expectation of change. Evidence of the changing nature of the student body, although sparce and unsystematic, was beginning to accumulate. The Commission's research and deliberations focused on the strong possibility that the differences during the 1970's between criminal justice and non-criminal justice students have become minimal. Criminal justice students should be viewed like other college students. They have the same strengths, weaknesses, needs, interests, and problems as other college students. Criminal justice education needs to reorient itself to the idea of the similarities, not the dissimilarities, of criminal justice students and other college students. Unless a reorientation takes place, criminal justice education will be out of touch with its changing students and will be providing them with an education reflecting an inappropriate set of low expectations.

Before criminal justice students can be assessed, however, the goals of an educational program must be understood. Bowen defines several principles that contribute to the definition of the goals of higher education:

> The whole person. Education should be directed toward the growth of the whole person through the cultivation, not only of the intellect and of practical competence, but also of the affective disposition, including the moral, religious, emotional, social, and aesthetic aspects of the personality.
> Individuality. A second widely held principle is that

education should take into account the uniqueness
of individuals, and this should help each person
develop according to particular characteristics and
potentialities.

Accessibility. A third principle is that higher education should be readily and widely accessible to persons of a broad range of abilities, circumstances,
and ages. This represents a fairly recent extension
of the older idea of the quality of opportunity, which
was usually based on a somewhat narrow conception of the content and purpose of higher education
and on the assumption that only a limited number of
persons could benefit from it (pp. 33-37).

From these principles, Bowen identified specific goals of
education: cognitive learning, affective development, and practical competence. If these three goals were achieved, the ingredients for the development of a student's total personality
would be present. In varying combinations--reflecting individual differences and personal qualities--these are the goals
to which many educators aspire for their students (Bowen,
1977, p. 39).

Given Bowen's goals for higher education, an understanding
of the changing nature of the student body can begin. Since
World War II two changes have affected the composition of
the students interested in criminal justice. First, the nation
witnessed a move towards universal education (Sandeen, 1976,
p. 36). As the educational system tried to provide the opportunity of college for all, severe problems developed. Jencks and
Riesman (1968, p. 286) observed several emerging dichotomies
between public and private schools, lower and middle class,
black and white. The inexpensive, less rigorous public colleges
created student bodies "more socially heterogeneous than the
private ones."

Second, between 1950 and 1980, a dramatic increase in
federal and agency funding occurred for higher education. The
G.I. Bill after World War II enabled many veterans to attend
college who could never have done so previously; enrollments
increased, and the student body diversified. After the Vietnam
War, veterans came to college with government financial support, and their enrollment changed the character of many
undergraduate classrooms.

Vietnam veterans have demonstrated a strong practical motivation in their academic programs. Many

> of them are older, of course, and have families, and
> they see the undergraduate degree primarily as a
> means to an economic end (Sandeen, 1976, p. 42).

College education became for many, a way to prepare for a
career or to advance in a career.

The criminal justice student came to be recognized as a practically motivated, grant supported, older individual. Many
criminal justice programs had been established with part-time,
inservice students who seemed similar to other commuter
undergraduates. Some have argued that the acceptance of inservice students had lowered entrance requirements and increased student enrollments. As Riddle (1977, p. 18) observed,
"Too many college administrators saw police education as an
opportunity to attract significant or even large numbers of
students, at relatively low cost."

As the number of preservice students increased, critics tended to focus on the quality of students in terms of their secondary preparation and their ability to maintain a good grade
point average in other courses. They viewed criminal justice in
the college or university as a relatively easy course of study,
which attracted, in the words of one critic, "The jocks and the
slow learners." Similar charges were leveled at sociology in the
1960's.

Goldstein (1977, p. 295) stated that the general growth of
criminal justice as a field of study perhaps reflected an attempt by students to "escape from more rigorous and demanding courses of study." Others have noted that police-oriented
programs are viewed as the new "safe and easy" courses in
higher education, thereby implying that they would be attractive to students of poor ability and motivation (Sherman,
1978, p. 158).

Like the G.I. Bill, L.E.E.P. funding probably contributed
more to enrollment size than either relaxed standards or the
wishes of academe. It has certainly upset the "balance of
power" among disciplines. A primary recommendation of the
President's Commission on Law Enforcement and the Administration of Justice, L.E.E.P. began funding in 1967 and
enabled a large number of students to enter college. To many,
the motivation of students appeared to be solely financial; going to school was seen as a part-time job (see Hall, 1977, cited
in Sherman, p. 148). Yet, the criminal justice student of the
1980's rarely conforms to those stereotypes.

During the 1960's and 1970's, a transition from part-time,

inservice students to full-time, preservice students occurred. Although the estimates of full- and part-time students vary from program to program and state to state, the number of inservice students certainly decreased dramatically. Indeed, a trend may be emerging toward an increasing number of "nonservice" students, especially at liberal arts institutions.

According to the *Criminal Justice Directory*, (1978, p. 13), almost 200,000 students are majoring in criminal justice. Because the growth of criminal justice as a field of study has been rapid, relatively little is known about the characteristics and aspirations of students enrolled in courses. The lack of comprehensive information about students suggests the need for a systematic inquiry into three criticisms directed at criminal justice students: 1. The view of educational participation as a means of increasing current income, 2. The view of criminal justice majors as individuals who seek an "easy" academic experience, 3. The view of criminal justice education as an exercise to generate credits by administrators who want to increase funding.

Early surveys of inservice students funded by L.E.E.P. provide the only available statistical profile of a significant number of students studying for criminal justice careers. The surveys found L.E.E.P. students to be male (90%), white (84%), and married (72%). Ninety-six percent were 25 years or older, and more than a fourth of them were more than 40 years old. Yet, as Sherman has noted, these data are not representative of preservice students, and a sudden increase in the percentage of preservice, non-service students was to occur and is verifiable (Sherman, 1978, p. 143). Although inservice students may have been predominant in the 1960's and 1970's, they were replaced by both preservice students and other interested non-criminal justice majors who were not inclined to seek employment in the field of criminal justice (Pearson, et al.). With the elimination of L.E.E.P., the number of inservice students has been decreasing.

In light of the changing characteristics of students in criminal justice education, the purpose of general education and of criminal justice education in particular needs to be rethought. In addition to inservice, preservice, and non-service students, two groups--women and minorities--have affected various programs (see Kuykendall and Hernandez, 1975, p. 112).

Because the majority of inservice students attending colleges in the 1960's had come from law enforcement agencies, the emphasis of most early criminal justice programs had been toward a law enforcement or police science curriculum. As noted in Chapter VI, that emphasis shifted toward a more systemic approach to criminal justice, because the increased number of preservice students were interested in a broad range of careers in criminal justice and because a young professoriate developed broad interests.

Very limited research has examined the expectations of students in criminal justice education. A 1973 survey of inservice L.E.E.P. students enrolled at the University of Southern California revealed that 57% of the respondents indicated a desire to become chief police administrators, and 24% stated that they aspired to the rank of captain. Hall (1977) found that many inservice law enforcement officers went to college apparently for the immediate salary increases. Sherman reported that most individuals testifying at regional public forums of the National Advisory Commission on Higher Education for Police Officers said they were going to college to improve their chances of being promoted to a supervisory rank. None mentioned improving their performance as police officers, nor did they mention learning for its own sake. Some officers stated that their ultimate goal in pursuing a college education was to leave police work (Sherman, 1978, pp. 146-147). Another survey by Tenney found that 37% of the respondents who had been employed in law enforcement at the time of their graduation from college (1962-1970) had left law enforcement by 1971 (Tenney, 1971, p. 60). Anderson (1978) found that many officers were apparently going to college for relaxation, therapy, and an escape from the rigors of police work.

Because most research conducted on criminal justice students has been limited by both the data and the orientation of the researchers, the Joint Commission undertook a study of students enrolled in criminal justice classes in 21 different programs. The data have been analyzed to determine who enrolled in criminal justice classes and what the real and perceived differences, if any, may be between criminal justice majors and non-majors in these classes.

Table IX-1 summarizes some of the demographic characteristics of the students surveyed. The data in Table IX-1 reveal that nearly two-thirds (64.6%) of the students enrolled were 22 years old or younger and that more than three-fourths (79.8%) of the students were enrolled full time. When criminal justice majors are compared with non-criminal justice majors, little difference is seen in their status. Table IX-2 demonstrates that the criminal justice major differs little

TABLE IX-1
SELECTED DEMOGRAPHIC AND EDUCATIONAL
CHARACTERISTICS OF STUDENTS ENROLLED IN
CRIMINAL JUSTICE CLASSES

Demographic/Educational Characteristics		N	%
Ethnicity	White	1264	76.0
	Non-white	399	24.0
	Total	1663	100.0
Gender	Male	1011	60.8
	Female	651	39.2
	Total	1663	100.0
Age	22 or less*	1075	64.6
	23 or more	588	35.4
	Total	1663	100.0
Student Status	Full-time	1327	79.8
	Part-time	336	20.2
	Total	1663	100.0
Class Rank	Freshman	515	31.3
	Sophomore	443	26.8
	Junior	368	22.4
	Senior	272	16.5
	Graduate	47	2.9
	Total	1645	100.0
Major Field of Study	Criminal Justice	1041	62.6
	Non-Criminal Justice	622	37.4
	Total	1663	100.0

'For a rationale for age breakdown, see A. Sandeen (1976, p. 36). "Students" have generally been largely thought to be persons between the ages of 18 and 22 who are engaged in full-time academic pursuits.

TABLE IX-2
STUDENT STATUS BREAKDOWNS BETWEEN TOTAL
SAMPLE AND CRIMINAL JUSTICE MAJORS

Total Characteristics		% of CJ Majors	% of Sample
Living arrangement	On campus	12.1	16.9
	Off campus	87.9	83.1
	Total	100.0	100.0
Student status	Full-time	74.9	79.8
	Part-time	25.1	20.2
	Total	100.0	100.0
Employment status	Full-time	39.7	29.3
	Part-time	29.7	35.7
	Unemployed	30.6	35.0
	Total	100.0	100.0
Current employment in criminal justice agency	Yes	26.3	18.1
	No	73.7	81.9
	Total	100.0	100.0

from the total sample in living arrangements and enrollment status. Although more criminal justice majors were employed full time than students of the total sample (39.7% vs. 29.3%), the figures for part-time employment for each group are almost reversed (29.7% vs. 35.7%); the figures for students not employed at all differ by less than 5%. The data indicate that a relatively high proportion of students enrolled in criminal justice courses and employed in a criminal justice agency are not majoring in criminal justice. Perhaps these inservice non-criminal justice majors enroll in criminal justice courses because of interest in work-related subject matter or because the courses selected serve as "comfortable" electives.

Most interesting is the finding that only approximately a fourth of criminal justice majors were actually employed in a criminal justice agency at the time of the survey (26.3%). The percentage might be expected to be higher than it is (18.1% for the entire sample), but it hardly supports the view that inservice students are a majority in criminal justice classes.

The Student Survey measured the students' own views of their high school and college G.P.A.'s, as well as their perceptions of their rankings in their class and university. In their self-assessments, criminal justice majors appeared very similar to the sample as a whole, with rarely more than a percentage point difference between the majors and the sample. Like most students, criminal justice majors perceived themselves as average students in high school and college, generally earning B grades. They also saw themselves as being slightly above the average level of their peers in both the classroom and within the university. Table IX-3 provides these data.

One difference between criminal justice majors and the sample as a whole was their reason for enrolling in criminal justice classes. As Table IX-4 indicates, more criminal justice majors saw the classes as important to their present or future jobs, whereas a greater proportion of the entire sample enrolled in criminal justice courses because of interest in the subject matter.

The data from the survey should begin to dispel most reservations about the relative abilities of criminal justice undergraduates. Both Goldstein (1977) and Sherman (1978) describe a general public doubt about the goals and expectations of preservice criminal justice majors. These critics perceive preservice students in a "new vocationalism," which is less demanding than other fields of study (Goldstein, 1978,

TABLE IX-3
COMPARATIVE SELF-ASSESSMENTS OF ACADEMIC
ABILITIES BETWEEN CRIMINAL JUSTICE MAJORS AND
THE ENTIRE SURVEY SAMPLE

Standard		% Majors	% Entire Sample
High School GPA	A	8.0	9.4
	A- B+	23.2	25.1
	B	27.2	26.9
	B- C+	23.5	22.1
	C	15.2	13.7
	C- D+	2.7	2.6
	D or lower	0.2	0.2
University-GPA	A	6.1	5.7
	A- B+	23.0	21.3
	B	27.3	27.7
	B- C+	26.5	26.6
	C	15.3	16.1
	C- D+	1.6	2.4
	D or lower	0.2	0.2
Class aptitude			
Well below average	1	———	0.1
	2	0.6	0.6
	3	0.4	0.5
	4	1.7	2.0
	5	9.1	9.8
Average	6	24.6	26.0
	7	23.0	22.6
	8	27.1	26.2
	9	10.6	9.5
Well above average	10	2.9	2.7
University aptitude			
Well below average	1	———	———
	2	0.3	0.3
	3	0.8	1.0
	4	3.3	3.8
	5	12.7	13.8
Average	6	30.4	30.6
	7	24.0	23.6
	8	20.8	19.9
	9	6.6	6.1
Well above average	10	1.2	1.0

TABLE IX-4
REASONS FOR ENROLLING IN CRIMINAL JUSTICE COURSES;
CRIMINAL JUSTICE MAJORS COMPARED WITH ENTIRE SAMPLE

Reasons	% of C.J. Majors m=1,041	% of Entire Sample m=662
Job related	21.9	17.7
Career preparation	53.9	42.0
Interesting course	19.6	33.3
Ease of course	0.6	1.0
Peer persuasion	0.5	1.0
Other reasons	3.5	5.0
Totals	100.0	100.0

TABLE IX-5
STUDENT PERCEPTION OF THE DIFFICULTY OF
CRIMINAL JUSTICE COURSES

Perceived level of difficulty in comparison with non-criminal justice courses	N	%
Same	1081	69.7%
More Difficult	249	16.1%
Less Difficult	220	14.2%
Total	1550	100.0%

p. 158). Sherman describes preservice students as motivated less by any cultural or social predisposition and more by a simple desire to obtain a degree easily (Sherman, 1978, p. 158).

With this criticism in mind, the Joint Commission's Student Survey queried students on the relative difficulty of criminal justice courses, compared with other courses. Most students (69.7%) considered criminal justice courses on an academic par with other courses they had taken; 16.1% thought the courses more difficult, 14.2%, less difficult. This data tend to refute the view that criminal justice courses are taken by students looking for "easy" classroom work.

The Student Survey also compared criminal justice majors with non-majors to assess their relative degree of general educational preparation. Both sets of students were asked to indicate the number of courses they had taken in the humanities, natural sciences, social sciences, and English. Of the criminal justice majors, 40% reported taking five or more social science courses, compared with 25.4% taken by non-majors. However, both majors and non-majors showed a great disinterest in humanities courses; 23.4% of majors and 23.2% of non-majors reported taking no humanities offerings.

This data may dispel the myth that criminal justice majors are poorly educated undergraduates, who over-specialize in criminal justice courses. They may also indicate more about the university requirements for the broad distribution of credits for general education and less about the personal preferences of the students. The very close correlation of kinds of courses taken by majors and non-majors implies that both groups of students were subject to distribution requirements over which they had little control, regardless of major. If so, those institutions should continue to demand of their criminal justice majors the same commitment to general education demanded of all other majors.

A large majority of all students, regardless of major, have decided to live off campus, and their decision only reinforces the "commuter school" aspect of their colleges in general and of criminal justice majors in particular. Of the colleges sampled in this survey, 40% were community and junior colleges. Between one-fifth to one-fourth of the students are part-time students, although statistics indicate that approximately two-thirds of them are employed either full or part time. A slightly higher number of criminal justice majors were commuters and part-time students, although the statistics did reveal that proportionately more of them were employed full time.

TABLE IX-6
NUMBER OF GENERAL EDUCATION COURSES COMPLETED FOR

Number of Courses	Humanities				Natural Sciences				Social Sciences				English			
	C.J.		Non C.J.		C.J.		Non C.J.		C.J.		Non C.J.		C.J.		Non C.J.	
	N	%	N	%	N	%	N	%	N	%	N	%	N	%	N	%
0	244	23.4	144	23.2	207	19.9	117	18.8	46	9.2	71	11.4	130	12.5	94	15.2
1	178	17.1	151	24.3	195	18.7	113	18.2	67	6.4	86	13.7	150	14.4	123	19.8
2	212	20.4	111	17.8	237	22.8	154	24.7	131	12.6	102	16.3	293	28.1	202	32.5
3	174	16.8	89	14.3	192	18.5	111	17.8	159	15.3	121	19.4	210	20.2	80	12.8
4	103	9.8	56	9.1	112	10.7	52	8.4	175	16.8	85	13.8	146	14.0	67	10.7
5 or more	130	12.5	70	11.3	98	9.4	75	12.1	413	39.7	157	25.4	112	10.8	56	9.0
Totals	1041	100.0	622	100.0	1041	100.0	622	100.0	1041	100.0	622	100.0	1041	100.0	622	100.0

Many critics, most notably Sherman (1978), have lamented the state of the part-time, commuter student, and the Joint Commission believes that the quality of education could be greatly improved by increasing the number of full-time, residency based programs for both inservice and preservice students. These full time, residency programs would give criminal justice students equal access to all student services. They would also, by keeping students on campus, encourage interaction with a diverse population, thereby complementing the in-class learning experience and exposing criminal justice students to the full range of collegiate life.

The Joint Commission's recommendations might also affect the career aspirations and expectations of criminal justice students. The Student Survey was designed to assess students' future aspirations and to assess the student commitment to criminal justice as a field of study and as a profession. The survey revealed that criminal justice majors were very concerned with the practical relevance of their courses of study to career advancement. Although they valued the courses they did take, they also strongly preferred specific courses of a very practical nature. Majors felt that the general progress and goals of education should favor practical preparation over theoretical instruction. However, few undergraduate students--particularly community college students--historically have found theoretical courses to be of interest or relevance, regardless of major.

Criminal justice majors were asked to identify the kinds of careers they wanted for themselves (Table IX-7). More than one-fourth (27.7%) identified policing as their future careers; 15% indicated corrections; 10.2% identified law. This data imply several future problems. The National Manpower Survey (1976) found a decline in the availabilty of law enforcement jobs but a substantial growth in the number of future corrections jobs. If the survey is correct, then the expectations of students in the survey will be unfulfilled. The Commission believes, therefore, that criminal justice programs owe students a reasonable assessment of their future employment in their preferred professions. Departmental counseling may be useful in interesting students in various careers and in directing them towards careers in which a definite need and good chance of employment exists. Few students saw employment opportunity in teaching (1.9%), and research and planning (2%). This data indicate little student interest toward the theoretical aspects of their majors and little motivation to

TABLE IX-7
CAREER PLANS FOR CRIMINAL JUSTICE MAJORS

Area of Career Interest	N	%
Law Enforcement	445	27.7
Corrections	240	15.0
Law	164	10.2
Courts	62	3.9
Private Security	46	2.9
Research Planning	32	2.0
Teaching	31	1.9
Other	584	36.4%
Totals	1604	100.0%

become teachers or researchers in the field.

Only 2.9% of the students sought careers in private security. That percentage reveals a sharp disparity between what is clearly a growing career field and the lack of qualified individuals to fill new positions. It also reinforces the findings of the survey of criminal justice majors into specific types. Of all the criminal justice majors, only 7% identified themselves as concentrating on security. However, more "private police" are working primarily in security positions than are public sworn officers.

A profile of criminal justice students is beginning to emerge. They seem to want professional careers in the criminal justice system, rather than in higher education or research. Although almost three-fourths of the sample (72%) indicated a desire to do graduate work most of this group sought only a terminal M.A. (43.6%) or wanted to attend law school (28.3%) (Table IX-8). The apparently high level of commitment to graduate

TABLE IX-8
GRADUATE SCHOOL OPTIONS FOR
CRIMINAL JUSTICE MAJORS

Intending to attend graduate school	N	%
Yes	786	72.0
No	306	28.0
Total	1092	100.0
Type of graduate degree:		
M.A./M.S. in crime-related field	343	43.6
M.A./M.S. in non-crime-related field	60	7.6
Ph.D. in crime-related field	93	11.8
Ph.D. in non-crime-related field	14	1.8
J.D. (law school)	223	28.3
Other	53	6.9
Total	787	100.0

study in the field is qualified by the very specific nature of that study; "over a thousand of them are aiming for a doctorate" is rhetorically misleading (Sherman, 1978, p. 143). The National Student Survey indicates that most students view graduate work, like undergraduate work, as pre-professional training. Motivation to learn has, as always, become motivation to earn, and criminal justice educators might be both flattered and chagrined to learn that more than one-fourth of the undergraduates view their majors as a viable pre-law program. This further reflects a need for adequate counseling of students by faculty members.

To the final question in the National Student Survey--"To what extent do you agree with the following statement: Colleges and universities should emphasize practical job related skills more than the understanding of major issues and theoretical concepts" --students responded (Table IX-9) by overwhelmingly supporting the view that abstract education is a way of preparing for a career, rather than a means of developing the mind. Of the sample, 62% either agreed strongly or simply agreed with the statement; 17.7% either disagreed strongly or simply disagreed. Most disturbing is the large percentage (20.1%) with no opinion. As Sherman might state, the low percentage of intellectually motivated students would naturally lower the "conceptual content" of a curriculum. If little demand existed for a conceptually rigorous course of

TABLE IX-9
EXTENT OF AGREEMENT THAT PRACTICAL JOB RELATED
SKILLS SHOULD BE EMPHASIZED IN COLLEGE AND
UNIVERSITY EDUCATION

Opinion	N	%
Strongly agree	265	24.1
Agree	419	38.0
Undecided/no opinion	221	20.1
Disagree	158	14.3
Strongly Disagree	39	3.5
Totals	1102	100.0

study, a faculty could acquiesce by establishing the kinds of limited professional programs criticized by the Joint Commission in Chapters VI and VII (for the term "conceptual education," and related terms, see Sherman, 1978, pp. 72ff; 129ff; and p. 85, Table 6 for a table of "conceptual abstraction" levels).

A student commitment to professionalism accompanied a desire for tangible professional success. Not only was professional aspiration by students great, but their desired success was great as well. Almost all criminal justice majors indicated that they hoped for employment at or near the highest levels of criminal justice administration; they expected to be a police executive or a warden. When asked for their realistic appraisal of their employment during the next decade, the students still considered their chances of success great (see Table IX-10).

The "careerism" of the criminal justice major at the expense of interest in theory and method may be disturbing. Alarm at such careerism is probably best tempered by recognizing that most students probably are and have been very career oriented. The question may also be asked: How can the rank and file of law enforcement and corrections be filled if most future personnel aspire to high administrative positions? Surveys in the 1970's indicated that inservice students returned to school either to be eligible for promotion from the beat to the desk or to leave police work altogether (Sherman, 1978, pp. 147-174). The work of Trieman (1977) and Guyot (1977) also demonstrated that the new, administrative priorities fostered by advanced education denigrated the value of police work and created potential problems for police departments and criminal justice agencies (Sherman, p. 147). Finally, although applauding the ambitions of careerists who seek promotions, educators may wince at the evidence of either non-existent or inaccurate counseling of students on the realities of occupational advancement.

To preservice students, vocationalism can be not only professionally limiting but also premature and intellectually dangerous. As Sherman warns:

> A serious motivation to learn vocational skills at the undergraduate level might inhibit a more general learning experience. Students whose only interest is in the romanticized 'nuts and bolts' of police work may have nothing but anti-intellectual contempt for more abstract conceptual knowledge (Sherman, 1978, p.158).

TABLE IX-10
STUDENT JOB SUCCESS ESTIMATES

Estimated Success in Obtaining Job of Choice

	N	%
Successful	1020	92.9
Not successful	78	7.1
Totals	1108	100.0

		Desired level of level of achievement in 10 years*	Expected Level of Achievement in 10 years**
Entry level (e.g., patrol- man, correc- tional officer)	1	0.1	0.2
	2	0.5	0.6
	3	0.2	0.5
	4	1.2	2.8
	5	1.3	2.7
	6	3.3	6.7
	7	3.8	4.7
	8	10.5	14.2
	9	6.5	9.3
	10	17.1	18.0
	11	12.3	10.5
	12	14.5	11.3
	13	7.9	5.2
Highest level (e.g. execu- tive warden)	14	15.7	10.4
	15	5.1	2.8

*students were asked to identify their desired level of achievement in 10 years using a 15 point scale with 1 representing entry level and 15 the highest possible level.

**students were asked to identify their expected level of achievement

The Joint Commission has seen the need for a broadly structured, interdisciplinary curriculum, and it believes that students must be exposed to a variety of intellectual and pedagogic courses of study in their undergraduate education. The Joint Commission's student survey was an attempt to assess criminal justice students within the broad context of undergraduate education. Whether the data on breadth of course work describe student motivation or institutional requirements, they bode well for undergraduate majors. Criminal justice students are no longer "different" from their peers. They require--both intellectually and academically--equal treatment. The services offered to all students should not be denied to a minority, simply because of their major. To the Commission, criminal justice students, like criminal justice faculty, should be evaluated only on academic performance, rather than on age, experience or enrollment status. Like their faculty, criminal justice students should be as much a part of the educational environment as others; they should receive equal but no special treatment.

As the student population in America has changed between the 1960's and 1980's criminal justice students have also changed. Indeed, criminal justice students may be more representative of undergraduates than was previously thought. With a strong professional commitment, they are usually enrolled in a public institution, probably work at least part time, and invariably commute to their classrooms.

Since Sherman's study, L.E.E.P. and its influence has perceptibly declined. Less than one-fourth (23%) of the students in the Commission's survey reported receiving L.E.E.P. financing. How will today's students affect tomorrow's criminal justice system? Will there be fewer patrol officers and more administrators? Will the professionalization of students during their undergraduate lives forebode a future criminal justice work force less enlightened than it is bureaucraticized? Criminal justice educators must insure that criminal justice students receive undergraduate educations of breadth and scope. Whether inservice or preservice, full- or part-time, students should receive the opportunity to immerse themselves as fully as possible in the academic environment.

Chapter X

IMPLICATIONS OF A
QUEST FOR QUALITY

The development of criminal justice higher education in America has been haphazard at best. Fraught with politics, poor leadership, a lack of planning, and varying levels of acceptance within the academic community, criminal justice programs were frequently scorned by the agencies they were designed to serve. In many ways, criminal justice educators in particular and higher education in general put self interest before the need for a reasoned approach to the development of the discipline. Although many individuals were sincerely dedicated to the improvement of criminal justice education, many entrepreneurs viewed federal funding as a quick source of income. During the early history of criminal justice higher education, federal dollars flowed almost faster than institutions could spend them.

Many university administrators, along with any number of criminal justice agency personnel with graduate degrees, took advantage of the federal largesse. Most had virtually no understanding of the real needs of an emerging discipline or field of study. The professional literature urged that criminal justice personnel should have a college background, but very little in the literature addressed curricula, the preparation of students, or the interrelated, interdisciplinary nature of criminal justice. When educators in the field began to organize planning and development, many of the police science and corrections programs were redesignated as criminal justice programs.

If any standards existed, they were generally personal, reflecting individual desires rather than a collective notion of what criminal justice education ought to be. Some programs displayed quality, and many individuals saw the need for quality controls. Nevertheless, in most programs established in the 1960's, faculty members were hired due to whom they knew, rather than what they knew and due to their experience, rather than their academic credentials. Often the faculty in police science, corrections, or criminal justice departments came from a common background and experience, frequently from the same agency. The usual selection of faculty by a committee, a well accepted academic tradition, was virtually ignored as university and program administrators filled their classrooms often with unprepared students taught by underqualified teachers.

In some institutions, part-time faculty in criminal justice programs had the workloads equivalent to those of full-time faculty in other departments at the same institution. Programs were sometimes staffed only with part-time instructors, with only the department chairman as a full-time teacher. The student/faculty ratios rarely allowed a small number of students to attend a seminar led by a full-time teacher. Instead, students would gather in large lecture halls where listening could be tedious and learning difficult. Inexpensive ways to promote mass education of criminal justice personnel were sought by university administrators who hired part-time teachers for criminal justice programs while employing full-time faculty for other disciplines.

The number of faculty who had adequate credentials and who understood the academic environment was relatively small. Moreover, they were frequently scorned by agency personnel who fostered the controversy as to whether a teacher should have twenty years of agency experience or the traditionally accepted doctorate. The controversy continues, but probably both academics and practitioners now agree that theorists and practitioners should teach.

In the 1980's faculty members generally have better credentials than their predecessors, because criminal justice program administrators have taken the initiative to establish themselves as academics. Indeed, the primary thrust for change and the recognition of a need for better quality came not from the traditional academics but from the youthful, recently employed criminal justice faculty members.

However, the Joint Commission found a great many deficiencies that warrant *meaningful* change. A need exists not only for minimum standards but for a reasoned approach to the development of increasingly stringent standards. The quality of teaching in some programs is surpassed only by the lack of rigor and the poor quality of much of the research conducted during the 1960's and 1970's. Many faculty in criminal justice are not qualified to teach or conduct research, and surveys made by the Joint Commission raise serious concerns about the level of commitment to research among many criminal justice educators. As financial incentives have replaced intellectual rewards, fewer capable students are entering graduate school with hope of becoming college and university teachers. As the job prospects for those already in graduate school dwindle, the lure of more secure professions only contributes to the shrinking population of qualified and motivated future teachers.

Criminal justice, an emerging field, must set its standards high enough to attract the best and the brightest individuals. The pioneers of the field are being replaced by younger, better educated individuals who must build on the solid foundations and traditions that have been established in the 1960's and 1970's. Judgment and foresight will be needed to identify those issues critical to the future.

Of particular importance will be faculty development. Too few resources have been devoted to increasing the capabilities of faculty to teach and do research. Professional associations have been increasingly active in recent years, but a renewed commitment and better planning by them must occur if the quality of faculty is to be improved. Faculty must recognize that they have a scholarly responsibility to prepare themselves for pedagogic and personal development. Members of the Commission talked to hundreds of faculty members across the country and found that most of them were unfamiliar with the literature of the field and with their specialization. Faculty are teaching courses in police administration with no knowledge of the Kansas City experiments, the concept of split force patrol, or recent research on response time. Faculty with a specialization in corrections have little or no acquaintance with research on the death penalty, community based corrections, or the literature on decision-making in probation and parole. How can anyone develop conceptual and theoretical ideas, so important to higher education, without a familiarity with the research in the field?

The number of faculty who do not subscribe to the journals or other publications in the field is cause for great concern. Regoli and Miracle's study on professionalism revealed a surprisingly low level of journal recognition: no journal is published that all respondents recognized, and many journals were hardly recognized at all (Regoli and Miracle, 1980, Tables, 5, 6, 9, 12). The Commission's own study also revealed a comparatively low interest among criminal justice educators in reading journals or writing for them. Not only are many faculty members apparently unprepared to teach, but few of them evidence any interest in learning how. The field has a responsibility to rid itself of those individuals who view the academic world as a haven for retirement or as a way to obtain a three month yearly vacation. The many responsibilities of a faculty member are generally well defined on most campuses. The individual who chooses not to meet those responsibilities does not contribute to the field of study or to the improvement of criminal justice. A person who retires from one field or job to accept a faculty position should do so with the knowledge that a new career has been undertaken with full responsibilities.

In selecting faculty, the field has made virtually no progress in recruiting women and minorities. The record of affirmative action in criminal justice leaves everything to be desired, and it is unforgivable in a program related to justice. That no qualified individuals exist to teach criminal justice is not well-founded. Everyone in the field must take the responsibility of seeing that qualified women and minorities gain a welcomed place in criminal justice higher education.

The curricula of criminal justice have certainly changed with an increasing emphasis on the systemic aspects of the field. However, curriculum development is a constantly changing process, and a strong need exists to emphasize conceptual and theoretical issues over practical aspects. Where a decision has been made to teach a student, the teaching must be supported by the most recent research and data available. The faculty member who has used the same lecture notes for twenty years is corrupt and must not go unchallenged. Without new knowledge, the roots of education starve and die. Much more is known about criminal justice than ten or even five years ago, but unfortunately many curricula are based on obsolete information and faulty assumptions.

Criminal justice education has also witnessed a continuing change in the nature of its students. In the future, more and more entry level positions should be filled by college graduates. The future of criminal justice belongs to the students enrolled in its programs, and the field must recognize its responsibility to prepare them in the best way possible. The responsibility is not a small one, nor is it a responsibility that can be achieved without consistent planning and reflection. Student involvement in the educational development process can be extremely valuable, and the field must be willing to call upon students to challenge it and to challenge those agencies in which they will ultimately serve.

A large number of students within the general academic community are registering for one or two criminal justice courses for the purpose of general education. That criminal justice can be attractive to the non-major must alter the view of the curriculum's obligation to the student and the student's own responsibility to the class. As the audience for criminal justice widens, educators must broaden the scope of their work to make it apply and appeal to the general community of students and to society. National studies indicate that the public is very concerned with crime. Helping individuals to understand the criminal justice system should be a primary duty of any educator in the field.

The recommendations of the Joint Commission are generally addressed to individual department heads and faculty members who have responsibility for the quality of their programs. However, because the field will never achieve an acceptable level of standards without collective action, the role of the professional associations becomes critical. The Academy of Criminal Justice Sciences and the American Society of Criminology probably represent the majority of faculty who teach or conduct research in criminal justice. These two organizations, working together, have the capability of bringing about major changes in criminal justice higher education. A.S.C. and A.C.J.S. must also work together with other professional associations interested in criminal justice and criminal justice education. A cooperative effort among them should clarify many of the misunderstandings and perceptions of the field and its activities. Professional associations must also develop workshops and other training sessions for improving faculty. The programs at national conferences and regional meetings should reflect a sincere desire to improve quality within the field. Working together, professional associations should also be willing to help individual programs to establish peer review projects, to obtain consulting assistance, and to publish material concerned with the specific issue of quality in criminal justice education.

After much debate and discussion, the Joint Commission decided that the implementation of minimum standards must be decided by the field itself, probably through the professional associations. A.S.C. and A.C.J.S. should establish a joint committee representing the leaders in each organization. The committee should have as its mandate the development of a cooperative and concerted effort to develop a plan for standards implementation. The committee should also have the responsibility of working with other professional associations to raise the level of minimum standards. The dynamic nature of the field warrants continuous review over the coming years, if it is to be successful in implementing and refining its standards of quality.

BIBLIOGRAPHY

Abel, Elie. 1978.
"Liberal Learning: A Tradition with a Future." *Liberal Education,* 64; 2: 115-21 (May).
Academy of Criminal Justice Sciences: Criminal Justice Accreditation Council. 1976; Revised 1978, 1979.
"Accreditation Guidelines for Postsecondary Criminal Justice Education Programs."
Academy of Criminal Justice Sciences: Criminal Justice Accreditation Council. 1977; Revised 1979.
"Accreditation Procedures for Postsecondary Criminal Justice Education Programs."
Adams, Arvil V. and Joseph Krislov. 1978.
"Evaluating the Quality of American Universities: A New Approach." *Research in Higher Education,* V 8: p. 97-109.
Adams, Reed. 1976.
"Criminal Justice: An Emerging Academic Profession and Discipline." *Journal of Criminal Justice,* 4: 303-314.
Ainsworth, David. 1977.
"Examining the Basis for Competency-Based Education." *Journal of Higher Education,* 48; 3: 321-32 (May/June).
American Academy for Professional Law Enforcement. 1978.
"Ethical Standards in Law Enforcement." Developed as a consequence of L.E.A.P.S., Second National Symposium on Police Ethical Practice with Subsequent Amendments, June 26, 1973.
Anderson, David C. 1978.
"The Off-Duty Degree." *Police Magazine,* 1: 29-38.
Astin, Alexander W. and Lewis C. Solmon. 1979.

"Measuring Academic Quality: An Interim Report." *Change,*
11, 6: 48-51 (September).
Bailey, Stephen K. 1980.
"Going Cold Turkey on Higher Standards." *The Chronicle of
Higher Education,* p. 64, January 28.
Baldridge, J. Victor, David V. Curtis, George Ecker, and Gary L.
Riley. 1978.
Policy Making and Effective Leadership. San Francisco:
Jossey-Bass.
Barrow, David P. 1941-43.
Memorandum to Accompany Department Budget Recommen-
dations Biennium 1941-43. University of California at Berkeley,
School of Criminology.
Bennett, Richard R. and Ineke H. Marshall. 1979.
"Criminal Justice Education in the United States: A Profile."
Journal of Criminal Justice, 7: 147-172.
Berkley, George E. 1969.
The Democratic Policeman. Boston; Beacon Press.
Beyer, Janice M. and Rueben Snipper. 1974.
"Objective Versus Subjective Indicators of Quality in
Graduate Education." *Sociology of Education,* 47; 4: 541-557
(February).
Blackburn, Robert, Glen Pellino, Alice Boberg, and Colman O'Con-
nell. 1980.
"Instructional Improvement Programs." In *Current Issues in
Higher Education;* No. 1: p. 32-48.
Bowen, Howard R. 1979.
"Socially Imposed Costs of Higher Education." *Conflict,
Retrenchment, and Reappraisal: The Administration of Higher
Education.* Urbana: The University of Illinois Press.
_____. 1977.
Investment in Learning. San Francisco: Jossey-Bass.
_____. 1980.
"Our Mission for the Teachers: A Nation of Educated People."
Case Currents, 6; 4: 10-11 (April).
Brandstatter, Arthur F. and Larry T. Hoover. 1976.
"Systemic Criminal Justice Education." *Journal of Criminal
Justice,* 4: 47-55.
Brantingham, P.J. 1972.
"A Model Curriculum for Interdisciplinary Education in
Criminology." *Criminology,* 10: 324-37.
Braskamp, Larry A., Steven L. Wise and Dennis D. Hengstler. 1979.
"Student Satisfaction as a Measure of Departmental Quality."
Journal of Educational Psychology, 71; 4: 494-98 (August).
Bressler, Marvin. 1967.
"Sociology and Collegiate Education." In Paul F. Lazarsfeld,
William H. Sewell, and Harold L. Wilensky, eds., *The Uses of
Sociology.* New York: John Wiley & Sons.

Bridgman, Olga W., M. Calvin, M. Chernin, R. Craig, B. Fritz, J.W. Gullberg, J.D. Holstrom, A.M. Kidd. P.L. Kirk, H.L. Mason, T.D. McGown, J. Neyman, J.B. de C.M. Saunders, O.W. Wilson, and H.E. White. Mimeographed, undated.
    "*Criminology.*"
Broady, Maurice. 1978.
    "Down with Academic Standards." *New University Quarterly* 33: 3-19 (Winter).
Brush, Stephen G. 1977.
    "The Search for Quality in University Research Programmes." *Social Studies of Science*, 7: p. 395-400.
Bynum, Timothy S., Jack R. Greene and Vincent J. Webb. 1981.
    "Apple Pie, Motherhood and Crime Control: An Exploration of Faculty Attitudes." Paper presented at November meeting of the American Society of Criminology, Philadelphia.
———. Jack R. Greene, Elizabeth M. Sebuck, and Vincent J. Webb. 1980.
    "The National Criminology/Criminal Justice Faculty Survey: Some Preliminary Findings." Paper presented at November meeting of the American Society of Criminology, San Francisco.
Carte, Gene E. and Elaine H. Carte. 1975.
    Police Reform in the United States; The Era of August Vollmer. Berkeley: University of California Press.
Chase, Alston. 1978.
    "Skipping through College." *Atlantic;* 242; 3: 33-40 (September).
Chickering, A. W. 1974.
    Commuting Versus Resident Students: Overcoming Educational Inequities of Living Off Campus. San Francisco: Jossey-Bass.
Conrad, John P. and Richard A. Myren. 1979.
    Two Views of Criminology and Criminal Justice: Definitions, Trends, and the Future. The Joint Commission on Criminology and Criminal Justice Education and Standards. Chicago: University of Illinois at Chicago.
Council of State Governments. 1975.
    "Judicial Administration Education and Training Programs." Lexington, Kentucky.
Culbertson, Robert G. and Adam F. Carr. 1981.
    Syllabus Design and Construction in Criminal Justice Education. The Joint Commission on Criminology and Criminal Justice Education and Standards. Chicago: University of Illinois at Chicago.
Day, Martin S. 1977.
    "A Funny Thing Happened on the Way to a College Education." *Humanist,* 37; 4: 22-6 (July/August).
Debro, Julius. 1979.

"Criminology and Criminal Justice Education in Historical Black Colleges and Universities." A paper presented at the annual November meeting of the American Society of Criminology in Philadelphia.

Deutsch, Monroe E. letter from; to Professor Frank M. Russell. 1945. University of California at Berkeley, School of Criminology. (July 19).

_____. letter from; to A.M. Kidd, P.L. Kirk, D.W. Wilson, Milton Chernin, A. Vollmer, and John Hicks. 1947. University of California at Berkeley, School of Criminology. (March 20).

DeZee, Matthew R. 1980.
The Productivity of Criminology and Criminal Justice Faculty. The Joint Commission on Criminology and Criminal Justice Education and Standards. Chicago: University of Illinois at Chicago.

Drake, Christopher. 1979.
"Nova University: The Controversial Dream." *Change,* 4: 16-18 (May/June).

Eskridge, Chris. 1981.
"A Survey of Selected Students of Criminal Justice: Developing Baseline Data." Unpublished manuscript; prepared for the Joint Commission on Criminology and Criminal Justice Education and Standards.

Felkenes, George T. 1980.
The Criminal Justice Doctorate: A Study of Doctoral Programs in the United States. The Joint Commission on Criminology and Criminal Justice Education and Standards. Chicago: University of Illinois at Chicago Circle.

Fincher, Cameron. 1979.
"Admissions Policies and Educational Standards." *College and University,* 55: 41-49, (Fall).

Fisher, James L. 1979.
"Where Are We Heading?" *New Directions for Higher Education,* No. 27. (Building Bridges to the Public.) 7, 3: 1-11.

Foster, J. Price. 1974.
"A Descriptive Analysis of Crime-Related Programs in Higher Education." Unpublished doctoral dissertation, Florida State University. Tallahassee.

Fox, James W. and Robert W. Ullman. 1976.
Volume III: Criminal Justice Education Manpower Survey. National Criminal Justice Consortium.

Fox, Vernon. 1968.
"Universities and the Field of Practice in Corrections." In Joint Commission on Correctional Manpower and Training, *Criminology and Corrections Programs; A Study of the Issues.* Washington, D.C., pp. 57-67.

Germann, A. C. 1957.

"Law Enforcement Education and Training in the United States." *Police Chief,* 24: 22-28 (October).

Goldstein, Herman. 1977.
Policing a Free Society. Massachusetts: Ballinger Publishing Company.

Goodman, Donald. 1979.
"Coordinated Curriculum and Criminal Justice Education." Paper prepared for the annual March meeting of the Academy of Criminal Justice Sciences.

Greene, Jack R., Timothy S. Bynum and Vincent J. Webb. 1981.
"Professional Identity, Patterns of Entrance and Attitudes towards the Field: A Study of Criminal Justice and Criminology Faculty." Paper presented at March meeting of the Academy of Criminal Justice Sciences, Philadelphia.

————. Timothy S. Bynum and Vincent J. Webb. 1982.
Crime Related Education: Faculty Roles, Values and Expectations. The Joint Commission on Criminology and Criminal Justice Education and Standards. Chicago: University of Illinois at Chicago.

Harris, John. 1978.
"A New Day for Assessment in Higher Education." *Educational Record,* 59: 268-82.

Hartle, Terry W., Joan C. Baratz, and Diane M. Crafa. 1979.
"Standard Setting: Do the States Care?" *Change,* Vol II, p. 56-58 (November/December).

Healy, Timothy. 1977.
"Can Quality Coexist with Equality in a Just Community?" *College Board Review,* 102; 8-11 (Winter).

Hefferlin, J. B. 1969.
Dynamics of Academic Reform. San Francisco: Jossey-Bass.

Hoffman, Dennis E., Joel C. Snell and Vincent J. Webb. 1976.
"Insiders and Outsiders in Criminal Justice Education." *Journal of Criminal Justice;* 4: 57-61.

Hoover, Larry T. and Dennis W. Lund. 1977.
Guidelines for Criminal Justice Programs in Community and Junior Colleges. Washington D.C.: American Association of Community and Junior Colleges.

Howe, Harold, II. 1980.
"Planning for the 1980's: The Context." *New Directions for Higher Education,* No. 30 (Managing Facilities More Effectively.) 8, 2: 1-5.

Hughes, John F. and Olive Mills, eds. 1975.
Formulating Policy in Postsecondary Education: The Search for Alternatives. Washington D.C.: American Council on Education.

Jacobson, Robert L. 1980.
"Campus Managers Shift Focus to Academic Quality." *Chronicle of Higher Education,* pp. 9-10, March 10.

Jencks, Christopher and David Riesman. 1968.
  The Academic Revolution. New York: Doubleday & Co.
Johnson, Carolyn. 1980.
  *The Literature of Higher Education in Criminology and
  Criminal Justice: An Annotated Bibliography.* The Joint Com-
  mission on Criminology and Criminal Justice Education and
  Standards. Chicago: University of Illinois at Chicago.
Joint Commission on Correctional Manpower and Training. 1968.
  *"Criminology and Corrections Programs: A Study of the
  Issues."* Proceedings of a seminar by the Joint Commission.
  Washington, D.C. (May).
Karabel, Jerome and Alexander W. Astin. 1975.
  "Social Class, Academic Ability, and College 'Quality'." *Social
  Forces,* 53; 3: 381-398. (March).
Karacki, Loren and John J. Galvin. 1968.
  "Higher Education Programs in Criminology and Corrections,
  Report of a Survey." In Joint Commission on Correctional Man-
  power and Training, *Criminology and Corrections Programs: A
  Study of the Issues.* Washington, D.C., p. 10-27.
Kerr, Clark. 1978.
  "Higher Education: A Paradise Lost." *Higher Education,* 7; 3:
  261-278 (August).
——. 1979.
  "The Administration of Higher Education in an Era of Change
  and Conflict." *Conflict, Retrenchment and Reappraisal: The Administration of Higher Education.* Urbana: The University of Illinois Press.
Kidd, A.M. letter from; to Acting President Monroe E. Deutsch.
  1945a. University of California at Berkeley, School of
  Criminology. (August 7).
——, letter from; to Professor Frank Russell. 1945b. University of
  California at Berkeley, School of Criminology. (August 11)
——, letter from; to Professor Frank Russell. 1945c. University of
  California at Berkeley, School of Criminology. (July 17.)
  , letter from; to President Robert G.Sproul. 1948. University
  of California at Berkeley, School of Criminology. (August 7).
Kirk, Paul L. letter from; to Provost M.E. Deutsch. 1946a. University
  of California at Berkeley, School of Criminology. (July 18).
——, letter from; to President Robert G. Sproul. 1946b. University
  of California at Berkeley, School of Criminology. (July 18).
——, memorandum from; to President Robert C. Sproul. 1946c.
  University of California at Berkeley, School of Criminology. (July).
——, letter from; to Colonel O.W. Wilson. 1947. University of
  California at Berkeley, School of Criminology. (May 22).
Kuykendall, Jack L. 1977.
  "Criminal Justice Programs in Higher Education--Course and
  Curriculum Orientations." *Journal of Criminal Justice;* 5, pp.
  149-163.

————. and Armand P. Hernandez. 1975.
"Undergraduate Justice System Education and Training at San Jose State University: An Historical Perspective." *Journal of Criminal Justice*, 3: 111-130.

Larsen, Rolf W. 1974.
Accreditation Problems and the Promise of P.B.T.E. Washington, D.C.: American Association of Colleges for Teacher Education and the E.R.I.C. Clearinghouse on Teacher Education.

Lejins, Peter P. 1968.
"Content of the Curriculum and Its Relevance for Correctional Programs." In Joint Commission on Correctional Manpower Training, *Criminology and Correction Programs; A Study of the Issues.* Washington, D.C. p. 28-56.

Leonard, V.A. 1942.
"Educational Policy and the Police." *Journal of Criminal Law*, 33: 198-204.

————. 1972.
"Chinese Central Police College, A Unique Institution." *Police*, 16: 16-21.

Levine, Arthur. 1978.
Handbook on Undergraduate Curriculum. San Francisco: Jossey-Bass.

Loughrey, Leo C. and Herbert C. Friese Jr. 1969.
"Curriculum Development for a Police Science Program." *Journal of Criminal Law, Criminology and Police Sciences*, 60: 265-71.

Lynch, James J. letter from; to Professor O.W. Wilson. 1953. University of California at Berkeley, School of Criminology, September 27.

March, James G. 1980.
"How We Talk and How We Act: Administrative Theory and Administrative Life." From Seventh David D. Henry Lecture, University of Illinois, September 25-26.

Marden, Sherley. 1979.
"An Examination of Accreditation Standards in Four Areas: Business Administration, Social Work, Public Administration, and Criminal Justice." Unpublished manuscript prepared for the Joint Commission on Criminology and Criminal Justice Education and Standards.

Marg, Elwin. 1979.
"How to Sacrifice Academic Quality." *Improving College and University Teaching.* 27, 2: 54-56 (September).

Marsh, Richard F. and Hugh W. Strickler. 1972.
"College-University Curriculum for Law Enforcement Personnel." *Journal of Criminal Law, Criminology and Police Science*, 63: 300-303.

Mathias, William J. 1969.

"A Criminal Justice Curriculum for an Urban Society." *Police Chief,* 36: 16-18.
————. ed. 1972.
Report of the Standards Committee Volumes I & II. Academy of Criminal Justice Sciences. (November).
Mayhew, Lewis B. 1972.
"Jottings." *Change,* 4; 2: 57-58. (March).
Meadows, Robert J. 1978.
"Strengthening the Two-Year Curriculum: A Nontraditional Communicative Approach." *The Police Chief,* 45: 49-50.
Miller, Jerry W. and Olive Mills. 1978.
Credentializing Educational Accomplishment. Washington, D.C.: American Council on Education.
Misner, Gordon E. 1975.
"Accreditation of Criminal Justice Education Programs." *Police Chief,* 42, 2: 14-16 (August).
————. 1981.
Criminal Justice Studies: Their Transdisciplinary Nature. The C.B. Mosby Co.
Morn, Frank T. 1980.
Academic Disciplines and Debates: An Essay on Criminal Justice and Criminology as Professions in Higher Education. The Joint Commission on Criminology and Criminal Justice Education and Standards. Chicago: University of Illinois at Chicago.
Mushkin, Selma J. 1972.
"Public Financing of Higher Education." In Logan Wilson and Olive Mills, eds., *Universal Higher Education: Costs, Benefits, Options.* Washington D.C.: American Council on Education, p. 153-178.
Myren, Richard A. 1970.
"Education in Criminal Justice." A report prepared for the coordinating Council for Higher Education.
————. 1980.
"'Justicology': An Idea Whose Time Has Come." *The Justice Reporter,* 1, 1 (Fall).
National Association of Schools of Public Affairs and Administration. 1977.
"Standards for Professional Master's Degree Programs in Public Affairs and Administration.
National Manpower Survey of the Criminal Justice System. 1976.
Criminal Justice Education and Training - Vol. 5. Washington, D.C.: U.S. Government Printing Office.
Neary, Matthew ed. 1978.
Higher Education for Police. New York: American Academy for Professional Law Enforcement.
Olscamp, Paul J. 1976.
"Quality, Quantity, and Accountability." *Educational Records,*

57; 3: 196-202.

———. 1978.
"Can Program Quality Be Quantified?" *Journal of Higher Education,*
49, 5: 504-511.

Pearson, Richard, Theodore K. Moran, James C. Berger, Kenneth C.
Landon, Janice R. McKenzie, and Thomas J. Bonita III. 1980.
Criminal Justice Education: The End of the Beginning. New
York: The John Jay Press.

Pelfredy, William V. 1978.
"Innovations in Criminal Justice Education: The Professional
Approach." Paper presented at the November meeting of the
American Society of Criminology, Dallas.

Phelps, Lourn. 1977.
"The Relationship between the Agency and the College: The
Berkeley Experience." *Higher Education for Police.* The
American Academy for Professional Law Enforcement, p.
50-54.

Pierce, C. Allen. 1981.
'The Impact of Police Higher Education Programs on Values
and Attitudes of their Students." Unpublished manuscript
prepared for the Joint Commission on Criminology and
Criminal Justice Education and Standards.

Piven, Herman and Abraham Alcabes. 1966.
"Education, Training and Manpower in Corrections and Law
Enforcement." Source Book I. Washington, D.C.: Pilot Study of
Correctional and Manpower of the National Council on Crime
and Deliquency.

Porter, John W. 1975.
"Articulation of Vocational and Career-Oriented Programs at
the Postsecondary Level." In John F. Hughes and Olive Mills,
eds., *Formulating Policy in Post-Secondary Education: The
Search for Alternatives.* Washington, D.C.: American Council
on Education, p. 206-214.

Regoli, Robert M. and Andrew W. Miracle Jr. 1980.
Professionalism among Criminal Justice Educators. The Joint
Commission on Criminology and Criminal Justice Education
and Standards. Chicago: University of Illinois at Chicago.

Riddle, Donald H. 1975.
"Faculty and Curriculum Development in Criminal Justice Pro-
grams." Delivered at Conference on Key Issues in Criminal
Justice Doctoral Education, University of Nebraska at Omaha.
1977.
"Liberal Arts and Vocationalism in Higher Educational Cur-
ricula for Police Officers." Consultants Report to the National
Advisory Commission on Higher Education of Police Officers.
(Summary appears in pp. 229-230).

Riesman, David. 1976.
"Thoughts on the Graduate Experience." *Change,* 8; 3: 11-16
(April).

Riley, Gresham. 1980.
"The Reform of General Education." *Liberal Education;* 66, 3: 298-306.
Rudolph, Frederick. 1978.
Curriculum: A History of the American Undergraduate Course of Study since 1636. San Francisco: Jossey-Bass.
Russell, Frank M., letter from; to Acting President Monroe E. Deutsch. 1945. University of California at Berkeley, School of Criminology. (August 3).
Sagarin, Edward. 1980.
"The Egghead, the Flatfoot, and the Screw: Some Reflections on the Future of the American Society of Criminology." *Criminology,* 18: 291-301.
Sam, Norman H. 1979.
"Life Experience - An Academic Con Game." *Change;* II, 1: 7 (February).
Sandeen, Arthur. 1976.
Undergraduate Students Education: Conflict and Change. Lexington, Mass.: Lexington Books.
Sanoff, Alvin P. 1980.
"Reaffirming Intellectual Standards." *Educational Records,* 61, 2: 10-14.
Schott, Richard L. 1976.
"Public Administration as a Profession: Problems and Perspectives." *Public Administration Review,* 36: 253-259.
Sebuck, Elizabeth M. 1981.
"Ideologies of Criminology/Criminal Justice Faculty: A Descriptive Study." Unpublished manuscript, University of Illinois at Chicago.
_____. and Vincent J. Webb. 1979.
"Toward Minimum Standards in Criminology/Criminal Justice Education: A Report on Research Progress and Prospects." Paper presented at November meeting of the American Society of Criminology, Philadelphia.
Selden, William K. 1960.
Accreditation - A Struggle over Standards in Higher Education. New York: Harper and Row.
Senna, Joseph J. 1974.
"Criminal Justice Higher Education--Its Growth and Directions." *Crime and Delinquency;* 20: 389-397.
Sherman, Lawrence W. 1977.
"College Curricula for the Police: Who's in Charge?" Paper presented at the June Conference on Criminal Justice Human Resources Needs. Michigan State University.
_____. and Warren Bennis. 1977.
"Higher Education for Police Officers - The Central Issues." *Police Chief,* 44: 32-34.
_____. and The National Advisory Commission on Higher Education for Police Officers. 1978.

The Quality of Police Education. San Francisco: Jossey-Bass.
————. 1981.
The Study of Ethics in Criminology and Criminal Justice Curricula. The Joint Commission on Criminology and Criminal Justice Education Standards. Chicago: University of Illinois at Chicago.

Simpson, Antony E. 1979.
Accreditation and Its Significance for Programs of Higher Education in Criminology and Criminal Justice: A Review of the Literature. The Joint Commission on Criminology and Criminal Justice Education and Standards. Chicago: University of Illinois at Chicago.

Smith, Gerald W. 1980.
"Illinois Junior - Community College Development 1946-1980." Illinois Community College Board.

Sproul, Robert G., letter from; to Paul L. Kirk. 1947. University of California at Berkeley, School of Criminology. (March 5).

Stephens, Gene. 1976.
"Criminal Justice Education: Past, Present and Future."*Criminal Justice Review,* 1: 91-120 (Spring).

Sterling, James W. 1974.
"The College Level Entry Requirement: A Real or Imagined Cure-All." *Police Chief,* 41: 29-31 (August).

Stinchcomb, James D. Undated.
"Current Issues Associated with Baccalaureate Criminal Justice Courses and Curriculum." *Virginia Commonwealth University.*
————. 1971.
"*Opportunities in a Law Enforcement Career.*" New York: Universal Publishing and Distributing Corp.
————. 1973.
"East Central State College - Assistance in Developing a Criminal Justice Curriculum in a State College - Police Technical Assistance Report." Virginia Commonwealth University.
————. 1977.
"The Two Year Community College - An Assessment of its Involvement in Law Enforcement from 1966 through 1976 with Future Projections." *Texas Police Journal,* 25: 6-14.

Strecher, Victor G. 1973.
"Education and Training through the Criminal Justice Career Cycle." East Lansing: Michigan State University.
————. 1977.
"Integration of Instruction, Research, and Service of the Professional Education System." *Police Chief,* 44: 69-71.

Swank, Calvin J. 1972.
"A Descriptive Analysis of Criminal Justice Doctoral Programs in the United States," Unpublished doctoral dissertation,

Michigan State University.
———. 1975.
"Criminal Justice Education: The Dilemma of Articulation."
Journal of Criminal Justice, 3: 217-222.
Taylor, Sheryl S. 1980.
"Criminal Justice as a Profession in Higher Education: A Case for Women." Unpublished manuscript, University of Illinois at Chicago.
Tenney, Charles W. Jr. 1971.
Higher Education Programs in Law Enforcement and Criminal Justice. Washington, D.C.: U.S. Government Printing Office.
United States National Advisory Commission on Criminal Justice Standards and Goals. 1973a.
A National Strategy to Reduce Crime. Washington, D.C.: U.S. Government Printing Office.
———. 1973b.
Corrections. Washington, D.C.: U.S. Government Printing Office.
———. 1973c.
Police. Washington, D.C.: U.S. Government Printing Office.
United States Department of Justice, National Institute for Law Enforcement and Criminal Justice.1976.
The National Manpower Survey of the Criminal Justice System, Vol 5: Criminal Justice Education and Training. Washington, D.C.: U.S. Government Printing Office.
University of California at Berkeley, School of Criminology. Undated.
"Notes on a Criminological Curriculum."
———. 1939.
"Recommendations for the Development of a Criminology Program." Mimeographed. (November 20).
———. 1944.
"Memorandum on Police Administration and Criminology Program Development." (December).
———. 1945.
"Report of the Committee to Consider the Present Status of the Program in Police Administration."
———. 1946.
"Report of the Committee on Educational Policy on Criminology." Mimeographed. (December).
———. 1947.
"Report of the Committee Appointed March 20, 1947 to Consider the Report on Criminology of the Committee on Educational Policy."
———. 1959.
"Reply by the School of Criminology to the Cline Report." Prepared for the Advisory Council of the School of Criminology. (August 20).
Ward, Richard H. 1983.

"The Future of Criminal Justice Education and Standards."
Presented at the Florida Criminal Justice Educators Associa-
tions Eleventh Annual Conference, March 1983.
——. 1979.
"Criminal Justice Higher Education: Lessons from the Seven-
ties, Issues for the Eighties." Paper prepared for the Western
Interstate Commission on Higher Education for a June con-
ference on "Issues in Criminal Justice Education."
——. 1977.
"Developing Minimum Standards for Higher Education in
Criminology and Criminal Justice." Paper presented at
November meeting of the American Society of Criminology,
Philadelphia.
Watkins, Beverly. 1980.
"Two Groups to Continue Accrediting Law Schools." *The
Chronicle of Higher Education.* p. 4. October 14.
Webb, Vincent J. 1981.
"A Study of Criminal Justice/Criminology Faculty: The Na-
tional Faculty Survey." Unpublished manuscript, prepared for
the Joint Commission on Criminology and Criminal Justice
Education and Standards.
——. 1981.
"The Accreditation Controversy: A Search for Standards of
Quality and the Future of Justice Education." *Justice Reporter,*
1, 2.
——. and Richard Ward. 1979.
"Issues in the Development and Implementation of Minimum
Standards." Paper presented at November meeting of the
American Society of Criminology, Philadelphia.
Wegener, Charles. 1978.
Liberal Education and the Modern University. Chicago: The
University of Chicago Press.
Weisman, Jack and Richard Holgate. 1979.
"Flowers and Leaves and Bits of Bloodstained Switches:
Mistaking Standards for Tyranny in the Classroom." *Liberal
Education* 65: 478-83 (Winter).
Wilson, Logan and Olive Mills, eds. 1972.
Universal Higher Education: Costs, Benefits, Options.
Washington D.C.: American Council on Education.
Wilson, O.W. Undated.
"Recommendations Relative to the Expansion of the
Criminology Program." University of California at Berkeley,
School of Criminology.
——, letter from; to Dr. David P. Barrows. 1940. University of
California at Berkeley, School of Criminology. (September 20).
——, letter from; to Dr. David P. Barrows. Undated. University of
California at Berkeley, School of Criminology. (May 15).
——, letter from; to Professor Frank M. Russell. 1947. University
of California at Berkeley, School of Criminology (June 30).

_____, memorandum to Chancellor Clark Kerr. 1953. University of California at Berkeley, School of Criminology. (October 27).

Winthrop, Henry. 1978.
"How Much Are College Students Learning Today." *Peabody Journal of Education,* 55; 2: 75-81. (January)

Wolfgang, M.E. and F. Ferracuti. 1967.
The Subculture of Violence: Towards an Intergrated Theory in Criminology. London; Tavistock.

Wood, Robert. 1980.
"The Disassembling of American Education." *Daedalus,* 109, 3: 99-113. (Summer).

Zalman, Marvin. 1981.
A Heuristic Model of Criminology and Criminal Justice. The Joint Commission on Criminology and Criminal Justice Education and Standards. Chicago: University of Illinois at Chicago.

Appendix I
MEMBERS OF THE ADVISORY COMMITTEE

When the Joint Commission was in existence several members of the Advisory Committee were employed in new positions. This list represents those members of the Committee who were appointed in 1978 to represent their agencies or associations.

Leo Culloo
> *National Association of State Directors of Law Enforcement Training* and *New Jersey Police Training Commission*

H. Lynn Edwards
> *American Bar Association*

Katherine Gabel
> *Women in Criminal Justice*

Jack Goldsmith
> *National Association of Schools of Public Affairs and Administration.*

John W. Gunn, Jr.
> *American Society of Crime Laboratory Directors, Inc.*

Paul Hahn
> *American Correctional Association*

Lander Hamilton
> *American Association of Community and Junior Colleges*

Samuel Harahan
> *Institute for Court Management*

John Heaphy
> *Police Foundation*

Kenneth E. Joseph

Federal Bureau of Investigation Academy
Peter Lejins
    American Association of Doctoral Programs in Criminal Justice and Criminology
Leo C. Loughrey
    American Academy for Professional Law Enforcement
George Lowe, Jr.
    Western Interstate Commission for Higher Education
Susan Martin
    American Sociological Association and *Society for the Study of Social Problems*
Joseph Peterson
    Center for Research in Criminal Justice
Robert Powitzky
    American Psychological Association
Thomas Reppetto
    American Society for Public Administration
Dale Sechrest
    American Correctional Association
David Shapiro
    American Board of Forensic Psychology
Ira T. Silvergleit
    Forensic Sciences Foundation
Sheldon E. Steinbach
    American Council on Education
James Sterling
    International Association of Chiefs of Police
Martin Tapscott
    National Organization of Black Law Enforcement
Carl Tucker
    National Sheriff's Association
Ecford Voit, Jr.
    National Institute of Mental Health
Charles Wellford
    U.S. Department of Justice - Office of Attorney General
Hallem Williams
    Positive Futures, Inc.

Appendix II
LIST OF PUBLICATIONS

Conrad, John P. and Richard Myren
> *Two Views of Criminology and Criminal Justice: Definitions,
> Trends, and the Future*

Culbertson, Robert G. and Adam F. Carr
> *Syllabus Design and Construction in Criminal Justice Education*

DeZee, Matthew R.
> *The Productivity of Criminology and Criminal Justice Faculty*

Felkenes, George T.
> *The Criminal Justice Doctorate: A Study of Doctoral Pro-
> grams in the United States*

Greene, Jack R., Timothy S. Bynum and Vincent J. Webb
> *Crime Related Education: Faculty Roles, Values and Expecta-
> tions*

Johnson, Carolyn
> *The Literature of Higher Education in Criminology and
> Criminal Justice: An Annotated Bibliography*

Morn, Frank T.
> *Academic Disciplines and Debates: An Essay on Criminal
> Justice and Criminology as Professions in Higher Education*

Regoli, Robert M. and Andrew W. Miracle, Jr.
Professionalism Among Criminal Justice Educators

Sherman, Lawrence W.
The Study of Ethics in Criminology and Criminal Justice Curricula

Simpson, Anthony E.
Accreditation and Its Significance for Programs of Higher Education in Criminology and Criminal Justice: A Review of the Literature

Zalman, Marvin
A Heuristic Model of Criminology and Criminal Justice

INDEX